THE FAN FACTOR

20 SLAM DUNK SECRETS TO ENGAGE YOUR ONLINE AUDIENCE

MEREDITH OLIVER

For information or bulk orders, contact:
meredith@creatingwow.com or call 866-227-9769

www.CreatingWOW.com

Front cover design by Justin Cohen.
Cover layout and interior design by Adina Cucicov, Flamingo Designs.

ISBN 978-0-9848684-1-4

Also by Meredith Oliver

Click Power
Face Up to Facebook
Link Up with LinkedIn
Click! Social Media Strategy
Seven Deadly Sins of Social Media

For My Mom and Dad

TABLE OF CONTENTS

ABOUT THE AUTHOR

Meredith Oliver, aka "The Digital Diva," is an Internet sales and marketing expert. She is a professional speaker, author, and consultant.

Meredith is the founder and president of Creating WOW Communications, a full-service web marketing and sales training company. Creating WOW Communications works with a variety of industries including marketing for home builders, senior communities, apartment communities, professional speakers, associations and small businesses. Creating WOW delivers services such as website design, search engine optimization and social media marketing.

Meredith holds a Master's Degree in Corporate Communication and Technology from the prestigious Rollins College and a Bachelors of Arts Degree, majoring in Psychology, from the University of Central Florida. She has 10 years of Internet marketing experience developing websites and online campaigns for small and medium size businesses.

Meredith is also a professional speaker delivering keynote speeches, workshops, webinars, and seminars to a wide variety of audiences, including real estate, healthcare, education, association, insurance, technology and women business owners. She speaks most often to business owners, sales people and marketing professionals, and is a proud member of the National Speakers Association.

Meredith speaks at a number of regional and national tradeshows and conferences each year. Meredith's seminars are consistently standing room only and rated by attendees among the most popular, entertaining and educational seminars offered. She is one of the speakers in the nationally acclaimed "Rock Your Sales" rally which appears to sold-out audiences across the country.

Meredith's first book, *Click Power: The Proven System to Increase Sales*, was published in 2010 and is available online at www.CreatingWOW.com. Meredith is the author and host of several social media click-by-click tutorials: "Face Up to Facebook," "Link Up with LinkedIn," "Seven Deadly Sins of Social Media," "Click! Social Media Strategy," and a Social Media Boot Camp.

Meredith has numerous published articles in national trade publications and newspapers. Her blog, The Digital Diva Blog, (http://thedigitaldivablog.com) is popular among sales and marketing professionals.

Meredith lives in Raleigh, N.C. with her husband, son and two Shih Tzus.

ACKNOWLEDGEMENTS

I love being a fan. It's who I am. I love to cheer and root for the underdog. I love competition. I love winning and even losing. Special thanks to the artists, athletes, professional speakers, authors and others who put themselves out there on a daily basis and give us something to cheer about.

I learned how to be a fan from my mom and dad. They have been my unwavering fans since the day I was born. Always positive and encouraging, it's because of them I've never seen any task as too hard to tackle.

Allen Oliver must be acknowledged for being the "fan" prototype in the book. Allen, I knew on our second date I was going to marry you. I just didn't know what an incredible journey we were going to take together (or that you were going to wear "licensed apparel" for the rest of our lives).

Brittany Smith, you are an angel who was placed into our lives for a reason! The idea for the book started the night we went to see Bon Jovi together and it never would have actually materialized without your shepherding, encouraging and editing.

In my professional journey, I've been lucky to meet several incredible people who willingly formed the Meredith fan club. Special thanks to Kerry Mulcrone for all of the wit and wisdom you bring to my life. You are a natural cheerleader and I can feel you cheering me on from the snowy tundra of Minnesota every day. John Palumbo and Melinda Brody are my fan posse; we travel the country together in the "Rock Your Sales" roadshow and we cheer each other on at every event. This book would not exist without either of you. I am a better person because of you.

Love to all of you,

Meredith

PREFACE

I am a Bon Jovi fan. If Bon Jovi performs within 200 miles of my zip code, I go to the concert. I play their music when I am writing, cleaning and running (they are playing right now!). I wear one of my Bon Jovi T-shirts at least once a week. I have loved Jon Bon Jovi since I was 14 years old. I've been a fan of many things during my life, but none have outlasted my love for Bon Jovi.

Bon Jovi recently played in Raleigh and I was there. My husband asked me why I needed to go to another Bon Jovi concert since we just attended one the previous year. So, I asked him if we needed to watch another Miami Hurricane football game since we just saw one last week. He promptly bought the tickets!

The idea for *The Fan Factor* came to me at the concert. Between songs, the band thanked the audience for helping them attain 12 million fans on Facebook. I am one of those 12 million fans. **No matter how busy I am, what time of day it is, or how many deadlines I have, if I see a Facebook post by or about Bon Jovi, I stop and read it.** Why? Because I'm a fan! It hit me at that moment; I needed to write a book about how to properly engage an online audience. The key to successful online engagement is to give fans what they want.

You may not be a Bon Jovi fan (I can't imagine why not), but, I'm willing to bet, there is something or someone you drop everything to hear, read or learn more about. From cooking to comic books, music to movies, dogs to decorating, everyone is a fan of something. If you tap into your own fan behaviors you can learn a lot about how to engage an online audience.

I know a lot about being a fan. I grew up in a family of avid sports fans. My mom and dad are *huge* Florida Gator fans. My mom's family is from the Gainesville area and my dad and brother are University of Florida graduates.

My dad was a pastor. I remember one particular Saturday when I was growing up that the Gators were playing a big football rival and he didn't want to be interrupted during the game. He put the garage door down, closed all the curtains and turned off the lights in the parsonage (except for the television of course) so parishioners passing by or volunteering at the church (we lived next door to the church) would think we were not at home. He did not want to be interrupted by church business during the game!

It was an inside joke at church that if a member needed prayer, guidance or a shoulder to cry on, my dad was not available until the end of the game. After a big victory, he was known for wearing his Gator tie the following Sunday in the pulpit.

One year the Gators were playing in the NCAA Final Four basketball tournament. That same night I was participating in the Miss Polk County Scholarship Pageant, hoping to win a spot to compete in the upcoming Miss Florida Pageant, which was the state prelim for the Miss America Pageant. Miss Polk County was the last local pageant of the year; my last chance to win a spot at Miss Florida. After the pageant (I didn't win), I asked, "Where's Dad?" He was in the hotel lobby watching the Gators play in the basketball tournament! Apparently, he was sneaking in and out of the pageant whenever I wasn't on stage to check the score. Now that I'm a parent, I appreciate how much he really wanted to watch the game and not some silly beauty pageant. To his credit, every time I was on stage and looked in the audience, my dad was sitting there. He is a Florida Gators fan but he's a bigger Meredith Oliver fan.

Even today, if we are hanging out with my dad during a Gators football game, it's best not to talk during plays and don't block the television! If we aren't watching the game together, we don't call during the game because it could jinx the outcome.

Fan behavior was such a normal part of my childhood, it's no surprise that I went on to marry an uber *sports* fan. Seriously, my husband's degree of "fan-hood" makes my dad's football watching habits look like child's play. My husband's entire wardrobe consists of "licensed apparel." It is a major ordeal to persuade him to wear anything that doesn't have a huge logo emblazoned on it.

Football, basketball, car racing, golf, tennis, soccer, volleyball, cycling; the list could go on and on. During the Winter Olympics, he even watched curling! It's one thing to be into curling, but it's another thing to watch it on TV half a continent away when you've never even played it.

Last spring during the Masters golf tournament, he actually connected his laptop to a LCD projector and projected the Internet coverage onto the dining room wall while the televised coverage was on in the next room. He explained to me this set-up was the best of both worlds; the live Internet coverage and the delayed coverage with the commentators. This went on for four days until the tournament was finally finished late Sunday afternoon. I was very relieved to see it go.

My husband is also very passionate about politics. When he isn't watching sports on television, he is watching cable news. He only watches one particular channel. The few clothes he owns that aren't licensed sports apparel have political endorsements/slogans all over them. His car is covered in magnets and stickers. Sometimes I feel like I am riding in a billboard on wheels.

What I admire and respect about my husband's fan obsessions is his dedication even in defeat. It doesn't matter if his sports team is losing or his political party is not in power. He always makes time and supports his causes with his whole heart. Lucky for me, his intense fan behavior isn't limited to sports and politics. He has been *my* number one fan for thirteen years. He is a fan of our family and our son, which is so lucky for us. When Allen Oliver supports something, he goes all out!

The purpose of this book is to teach you how to grow your business by engaging your online audience in a way that turns them into fans. The advent of social media gives every business the opportunity to connect with customers and potential customers. You have an online audience. The question is: How engaged are they with you? Your customers are going to talk about you with or without your participation. Wouldn't you prefer to be a part of the conversation?

The purpose of this book is *not* to convince you to start using online marketing or *why* you need to spend money marketing your business. The time for that logic has passed. You know your business needs marketing to survive and common sense tells you the three "P's of Marketing" (print marketing, phone books and pagers) are dead and no longer produce results. Your own shopping habits are proof enough that consumers overwhelmingly go online to research products and services to buy.

The Fan Factor is for serious sales and marketing professionals who want to increase sales using Internet marketing. This book can help:

☞ The entrepreneur starting a new business who wants to build a legion of loyal fans willing to buy his/her products.
☞ The executive director of an association who wants to increase and retain membership with Internet marketing and social networking.
☞ The business owner and/or corporate marketing manager who wants the most exposure possible from a tight marketing budget.
☞ The salesperson who understands the importance of connecting online for prospecting, presenting, closing and follow-up.
☞ The social media manager who wants to develop an online community of followers who are active advocates of the brand message.

Above all, this book is for *you*. My goal is to teach you how to grow your business and reach new heights with Internet marketing done right.

PART I

THE PRE-GAME

*"You have no control over what the other guy does.
You only have control over what you do."*

A.J. Kitt
Alpine Ski Racer
1993 Bronze World Championship Medalist

WE CAN'T HEAR YOU

With 700 Facebook status updates per second[1], 200 million tweets per day[2] and 14.65 billion web pages in existence to date[3], consumers are overwhelmed by an avalanche of sales and marketing messages.

"Every two days we create as much information as we did from the dawn of civilization up until 2003," said Eric Schmidt, executive chairman of Google, at a technology conference in August 2010. "That's something like five exabytes of data." An exabyte is defined as a "unit of information or computer storage equal to one quintillion bytes."[4] In layman's terms, one exabyte of storage could hold 50,000 years of DVD-quality video."[5] *Whoa.* Let that sink in for a second.

Without a sound Internet marketing strategy, a compelling message and loyal fans who are eager to hear your message, your website updates, email campaigns, Facebook posts, text messages and tweets will blend into a deafening cacophony that sounds like Charlie Brown's teacher giving instructions for a pop quiz. Blah-blah-blah. Yaddy-yaddah-yaddah. Wah-wah-wah.

Consumers today are overwhelmed with media messages because the amount of media we consume per day is staggering. **An eMarketer study found the average time spent with all major media at 11 hours per day!**[6] Of those 11 hours, we spend 4 hours and 24 minutes a day watching TV and 2 hours and 35 minutes online. One of the biggest shifts in media consumption is the increase in time spent with mobile devices. "Time spent with mobile devices is rising faster than all other media. In 2010, consumers spent 28.2 percent more time with mobile devices."

We don't even have to be home anymore to consume media. We can consume it on the go with mobile phones and tablets (but hopefully not while driving!). Pew Research Center found that "35 percent of American adults own some kind of smartphone, and among adult mobile users that figure rises to 42 percent."[7] New McKinsey research found that 50 percent of US online consumers are "advanced users of smartphones, social networks and other emerging tools—up from 32 percent in 2008."[8]

How sure are you that your online customers can hear you? Is your message coming across loud and clear? Ask yourself these questions:

- ☞ How many "Contact Us" request forms do you receive each month from your website?
- ☞ How often do you receive a reply and/or order from an email campaign?
- ☞ How often does someone comment on your blog or "Like" your posts on Facebook?
- ☞ How often are your tweets re-tweeted?

☞ How many online sales do you average a month? Is that number continuing to grow?

☞ How often does your offline sales team report that a prospect purchased directly as a result of visiting your website?

If you are worried your message is not breaking through, don't worry. That's exactly what this book is all about!

WE HAVE POPCORN BRAIN

We spend so much time consuming media, especially online, because it feeds our brain the instant gratification, speed and unpredictability we crave. Some of us are so hooked we neglect offline tasks and relationships in lieu of being online. If this sounds geeky, pathetic or unreasonable, don't be so quick to judge. Answer these questions honestly:

- ☞ Have you ever felt compelled to check your email at a completely inappropriate time, just in case something important has come in?
- ☞ Have you ever forgotten or lost your cell phone and felt panicked until it was located?
- ☞ How often is your mobile phone further than arm's length away from you at any point during the day and night?
- ☞ How many computers, mobile phones, tablets, televisions and/or satellite radios do you own? Are there as many devices as people in your household or perhaps even more?

☞ Do you have satellite radio in your car or a USB connection for your MP3 player so you can listen to music or podcasts regardless of your location?

☞ How many channels are available in your cable television package? How often do you subscribe to pay-per-view or premium channels because the basic channels don't offer enough variety and choices?

☞ Do you subscribe to a DVD or online streaming movie service where you receive multiple new movies a month in addition to the cable movie channels available on your television?

Researcher David Levy calls this phenomena **"popcorn brain"** or "a brain so accustomed to the constant stimulation of electronic multitasking that we're unfit for life offline, where things pop at a much slower pace."[9] In this day and age we all suffer from a little bit of popcorn brain and it isn't a personality flaw. It's a biological imperative. Our brains crave stimulation and new information.

The challenge for sales and marketing professionals is to figure out how to leverage the popcorn brain phenomena into new sales. Let's face it: Your potential customers are distracted and overwhelmed. You need to work extra hard to get and keep their attention.

Do you remember the television commercial for the investment firm EF Hutton? The famous tag line was "When EF Hutton talks, people listen." EF Hutton wanted to hammer home that their message was so important and their staff members so knowledgeable, that it was worth stopping everything to listen.

Is your sales and marketing message so compelling, interesting, informative and credible that it's worth dropping everything to listen to?

WE ARE MEDIA MULTITASKERS

Not only do we spend a lot of time consuming media, many consumers pay attention to more than one media source at a time. Researchers call this "media multitasking." We wake up to our custom Pandora radio station on our iPhone, turn on our favorite cable news channel of choice, check our email and text friends (all before we hit the shower or have our first cup of coffee). Some of us even media multitask in the bathroom!

- ☞ Do you work on the computer with the television or radio on in the background?
- ☞ Do you check email on your phone during meetings when you should be listening to the person speaking?
- ☞ Do you monitor social network sites like Twitter or Facebook at work while you are answering email or doing other work on your computer?

☞ Do you use a social media dashboard application such as Hootsuite or Tweetdeck to monitor several social media sites in one place because you like the streaming effect of multiple windows at the same time?

☞ Do you watch television with a laptop or tablet in your lap to surf the web and check social networks? Is your phone also nearby?

☞ Do you own a DVR? When was the last time you watched a television commercial other than during a live sporting event or news program?

If you do any of these things, you are a media multitasker. It's not that you don't want to pay attention (in most cases), it's that you feel compelled to multitask partly because you have popcorn brain and partly because **there is so much information available we have little choice but to spread our attention among several media outlets at once and hope something sinks in**.

Wikipedia defines media multitasking as
> "Using TV, the web, radio, telephone, print, or any other media in conjunction with another. Also referred to as 'simultaneous media use,' this behavior has emerged as increasingly common, especially among younger media users, and has gained significant attention in media usage measurement, especially as a new opportunity for cross-media advertising."[10]

I first became aware of the term media multitasking in 2007 when I read it in an eMarketer.com article talking about the new phenomenon of media multitasking and the implication for marketers. "Researchers estimate that 25-30 percent of total media time is spent multitasking, and the more media a person consumes, the more likely they will consume several channels at once."

The bad news for sales professionals and marketers is that media multitaskers are not necessarily more connected, but more distracted. According to a study of media multitasking by Boston College researchers, multitaskers "placed in a room containing a television and a computer and given a half hour to use either device, people on average switched their eyes back and forth between TV and computer a staggering 120 times in 27.5 minutes—or nearly once every 14 seconds…"[11] With so much distraction all around us, a lack of concentration is bound to lead to mistakes. That's why your mom insisted you do homework with the television OFF.

The study also found that "multitaskers who think they can successfully divide their attention between the program on their television set and the information on their computer screen proved to be driven to distraction by the two devices." This particular study focused on the interaction between the computer and television; imagine what the numbers would look like if we factored mobile phones and tablets into the equation!

Given how distracted consumers are, you have two options.

1. *Fight for attention.* This is going to take money. A lot of money. You will need to stake out your territory in the marketplace and shout loud enough and frequently enough to stand out and be heard. This is the philosophy behind traditional "push" marketing. Consumers have grown weary and skeptical of invasive push advertising and that means you have to do even more to get their attention. It's expensive and becoming increasingly ineffective.

2. *Ask for as little attention as possible.* What? Have I lost my mind? Nope! With this option you attract or "pull" consumers to you because the message is about them. You also make it super easy to

access your message, products and services online with one click no matter how distracted a customer may be. This option seems counterintuitive because we are trained to dominate the conversation, talk about ourselves and keep the client's attention for as long as possible. But if you let go of traditional thinking and embrace *The Fan Factor*," you can "pull" customers in and increase your sales.

If you want to implement Option #2, your marketing will need to be one-click easy or it will demand too much time from your fans. Take the one-click test below.

Your Website:

- ☞ Can a visitor buy your product/service and/or find pricing and purchase steps with one click from the homepage?
- ☞ Can a visitor find your phone number, email address or physical address prominently displayed above the scroll on every page?
- ☞ Can a visitor chat live with a representative to find out information in real time?
- ☞ Can a visitor sign up for email updates and connect to your social media sites?

Your Business (Fan) Facebook Page:

- ☞ Can a visitor buy your product/service, search your catalog of offerings and/or chat live with a representative?
- ☞ Can a visitor sign up for email updates?
- ☞ Can a visitor connect with your other social media sites?

Your Blog:

- ☞ Can a visitor sign up for an RSS feed or email subscription?
- ☞ Can a visitor purchase your product or connect to more information about your product/services, including pricing?
- ☞ Can a visitor link to your website and other social media sites?

If you want valuable feedback about your online marketing, ask a teenager to surf your website, blog and social media sites and let them keep their mobile phone while they do it. They will text, talk and check social media sites on their phone in one hand and surf your sites with the other hand. At the end of the exercise, if he/she can tell you what you are selling, how to purchase it or how to find out more information, you've passed the one-click test.

BIG COMPANIES SPEND BIG BUCKS TO BE HEARD

To compensate for the avalanche of media messages and the distracted nature of most consumers, advertisers repeat their messages with a high degree of frequency and use a variety of formats. In one day it is entirely possible to see a Coke television commercial, drive by a bus bench with a Coke logo on it, tune into American Idol to see the judges drink from plastic red Coke cups, see a Facebook ad for Coke, view a newspaper insert with Coke for sale at the local grocery and go online to enter to win a Coke contest printed on the inside of the cap of your Coke bottle. With this much reach and frequency, Coke creates top of mind awareness and influences consumer buying decisions. Coke's marketing message can be heard loud and clear.

Coke, Nike, Pepsi, Walt Disney World, Target—all of these brands can afford pricey national television commercials, product placements and corporate sponsorships. If you are the owner of a small to medium size business, your marketing budget probably isn't large enough to invest in a national mass media campaign with enough reach and frequency to break through our popcorn brains and influence a purchase decision. And, if you are the chief marketing officer for a big company, is there a better, less expensive way to get the same results?

If you aren't a big company, what's your game plan? Just because you can't afford a Super Bowl commercial doesn't mean you shouldn't market your business. Aside from winning the lottery, what's your next move?

The good news is that while you may find it hard to compete with larger companies in print or broadcast advertising, online sales and marketing tactics are highly doable and extremely affordable. Some are even DIY (do-it-yourself) friendly if you have the proper training and tools. Internet marketing tools to consider include:

- ☞ Search engine optimization (SEO)
- ☞ Paid search marketing
- ☞ Social media
- ☞ Content marketing
- ☞ Email marketing
- ☞ Blogging

Until online marketing came along, you probably relied on local customers who knew your name and referred you through word-of-mouth. Today, if your online marketing is sufficiently *pervasive and persuasive*, you can use **"word-of-mouse"** to reach potential customers who have never heard of your brand name. With effective online marketing, prospective customers won't know the difference between your company and the big guys. You can look big, deliver big and, most importantly, *sell* big!

How do you get started? Make a list of everything you are doing to market your business and how much each item costs.

- ☞ What marketing tactics are you currently using?
- ☞ What tactics are producing sales?
- ☞ What tactics are not producing sales?

Add up the dollar amount you are spending on the tactics that are not producing sales. Shift those dollars to online marketing. Review the results in six months. Most businesses are so pleased with the results that they find even more dollars to put toward online marketing.

ENGAGED FANS ARE THE ANSWER

The key to overcoming your customer's popcorn brain and media multitasking is *not* to shout louder and more frequently than the competition. Do exactly the opposite. Turn down the volume on the overly "salesy" rhetoric, throw out the stuffy corporate brochures and delete those awful death-by-power-point 50-slide presentations. Instead, whisper. That's right, pull the customer or client to you with an authentic whisper designed to appeal to the needs, desires and goals of your target audience.

What would make your target audience stop and listen? How can you get your customer's attention and keep it long enough to make a sale?

The answer is what I call *The Fan Factor*: Engaged fans stop to hear your message no matter how busy they are.

The key word in that sentence is **engaged**. It's not enough to have fans. If you deliver a great product/service at a reasonable value, you will have fans. What you really need are **engaged** fans.

- ☞ *Engaged fans* are never too busy for your message. They make time to listen to your message and purchase your products/services.
- ☞ *Engaged fans* refer new fans. Word of mouth referrals are worth thousands of dollars of push advertising and cost far less.
- ☞ *Engaged fans* are repeat customers. They are loyal to your brand. As a universal business truth, it is easier and less expensive to sell more to your existing customer base than acquire new customers
- ☞ *Engaged fans* care about your success. They give valuable feedback on your products/services that will help you improve and/or invent new products/services.

Political campaigns offer excellent examples of how engaged fans produce results. In the political world, fans are referred to as the "base." The 2004 Bush-Cheney campaign demonstrated just how powerful an engaged fan base can be on Election Day. Prior to the 2004 election, the predominant political strategy was to focus on swing voters, defined by Wikipedia as "a voter who may not be affiliated with a particular political party (Independent) or not vote across party lines."[12]

In the PBS television special "Karl Rove—The Architect," Chief Campaign Strategist for Bush-Cheney 2004 Matthew O'Dowd talks about the decision they made to focus on mobilizing the Republican "Compassionate Conservative" base of voters instead of focusing on the independent swing voters. O'Dowd looked at the voter turnout from the 2000 election and discovered:

"…Independents or persuadable voters in the last 20 years had gone from 22 percent of the electorate to 7 percent of the electorate in 2000. And so [we concluded that]…93 or 94 percent in 2004…was already going to be already decided either for us or against us. You obviously [still] had to do fairly well among the 6 or 7 [percent], but you could lose the 6 or 7 percent and [still] win the election, which was fairly revolutionary, because everybody up until that time had said, 'Swing voters, swing voters, swing voters, swing voters, swing voters.'"[13]

How did the 2004 Bush-Cheney campaign mobilize voters? O'Dowd says the campaign looked at the mistakes from the 2000 campaign and made adjustments.

"[We focused on] much more person-on-person contact in individual communities. So much more building [a volunteer network] up, having an infrastructure where somebody could call into a neighborhood or precinct, to call up voters that they knew. In the past [direct] mail was not as emotional as it should have been, so the [direct] mail was more emotional. More actual, real phone calls, as opposed to what they call robo-phone calls, which are sort of robotic phone calls where you say, 'Go vote, go vote.' There were more people in a community that might know a list of 100 people that they could call—things like that."

The 2004 Bush-Cheney campaign strategy was effective and produced the desired result. However, it missed the mark in one critical area: how to utilize the Internet to engage fans faster and cheaper than traditional marketing.

That mistake was not lost on the 2008 Obama-Biden campaign. The Obama-Biden ticket was the first presidential campaign in history to truly harness the power of the Internet to engage the base. "Both candidates used the Internet to reach voters. But Team Obama mastered the medium early and exploited it to the hilt. Along the way, it changed politics—and government—perhaps forever."[14]

What did the Obama 2008 campaign do that was so effective? First, they built a social network of energized fans. In political terms, they built an "online base" of followers. Second, they regularly fed the fans with highly targeted, personalized online content, including:

- ☞ Text messages for younger voters.
- ☞ Email campaigns for older voters.
- ☞ Online ads targeted to the viewer based on past browsing history.
- ☞ YouTube videos.
- ☞ Blog posts.
- ☞ Online contests for donors.

What made the Obama-Biden ticket so much more effective online than the McCain-Palin ticket was the online base of followers. McCain-Palin, in an effort to keep up, started producing online videos, but lacked the grassroots network of supporters to take it viral. Think of it like a rock band performing to an empty stadium.

YouTube was one of the most effective tools for the Obama-Biden campaign because it allowed the candidates to communicate directly with the base in a very personal way without the filter of the national media. Since YouTube videos, unlike television commercials, are permission based (meaning the viewer chooses to watch it or not), fans felt emboldened and empowered to spread the message. The groundswell of support was overwhelming and resulted in record campaign donations. Obama-Biden fans weren't just passive "likely" voters; they were active advocates who contributed to President Obama's historic win on election night.

Imagine your business is a political campaign. Would you be looking forward to a big turnout on Election Day or worried the weather might keep lukewarm supporters at home?

1. On a scale of 1 to 10 (1 being low, 10 being high) rate the engagement level of your fans.
2. Set a goal to raise that number within the next six months and to raise it again within a year.

FORMULATE YOUR GAME PLAN

Take time to answer the following:

1. How do the five facts presented in this section impact your business?

_____

_____

_____

2. What did you learn from this section?

_____

_____

_____

3. How will you change your business based on this new knowledge?

_____

_____

_____

4. What first action step do you need to take to implement that change? When will you take that step?

_____

_____

_____

PART II

THE GAME PLAN

"Good teams become great ones when the members trust each other enough to surrender the 'me' for the 'we.'"

Phil Jackson
Former Los Angeles Lakers Head Coach
Most Winning NBA Coach of All Time

THE DNA OF A FAN

Ever asked an avid sports fan "What's the big deal, it's just a game, right?" Then you know the response is generally a blank expression and a shrug of the shoulders indicating you just don't get it. Their answer can't be put into words. It's a feeling embedded deep in the bedrock of their personality.

Psychologists and researchers have long studied the behavior of extreme sports fans and we can learn a lot about how to engage fans from their findings (even if you aren't a sports fan you are probably a fan of some other type of hobby, pasttime or entertainer and will relate to the research conclusions). A Bleacherreport.com article[15] outlines the following five reasons for extreme sports fan behavior:

Reason #1—Identity
Fans identify with the team. It is part of who they are. "Our sports heroes are our warriors," Robert Cialdini, a professor of psychology at Arizona State, said about sports fans. "This is not some light diversion to be enjoyed for its inherent grace and harmony. The self is centrally involved in

the outcome of the event." I know this is true from watching my dad and husband. They feel the outcome very personally as if they are on the field catching the game-winning touchdown. Ask a fan why he/she follows a particular team and, most of the time, the answer is "I don't know—I just always have" or "My dad/uncle/brother watched this team and I've been following them my whole life."

Much of the sense of identity is passed on through the generations. I didn't attend the University of Florida (UF) because I was fortunate to receive a full scholarship to the University of Central Florida (UCF), but I have always been and will always be a Gator fan. It's just who I am.

☞ Are you or do you know an extreme sports fan? Ask yourself or him/her, why do you support a specific team/ individual over other sports figures?

_____

_____

_____

_____

☞ When did your interest start? Why are you interested?

_____

_____

_____

_____

Reason #2—Self-Esteem

Because sports fans identify so strongly with the team, their own self-esteem can rise and fall with the success of the team. Psychologist Dr. Daniel Wann's research on avid sports fans found "that an intense interest in a team can buffer people from depression and foster feelings of self-worth." Conversely, researchers have also found that fans who experienced a team loss felt less optimistic about everything from "getting a date to winning at darts…"[16] For sports fans, the players are heroes who demonstrate bravery, courage and discipline, attributes which inspire fans to perform better, resulting in higher self-esteem.

Fans love to see the underdog team/individual win against all odds. We feel like if they can do it, so can we. And vice versa: When our favorite sports hero falls from grace, we question our own humanity and frailty. Your fans want to feel good about themselves and your brand is part of that equation.

☞ How do you feel when your favorite team/individual wins? What does it do for your day?

☞ How do you feel when they lose? How does that impact your day/week?

Reason #3—Escapism

Sports fans use sports as an escape from the daily grind. My husband told me on numerous occasions that he works hard all week so he can watch sports on the weekend. He says it transports him away from work and home demands. Just like old-fashioned soap operas, the world of sports is full of drama, controversy and surprise endings. Fans feed off of the emotion and conflict, temporarily forgetting their own problems.

But it's not all about the drama. It's also about the success. For those few moments, fans get to root for a cause bigger than themselves and hope for a positive outcome. Some male sports fans have taken the idea of escaping so seriously, they have a "man cave" or a room dedicated just for sports watching.

☞ Do you have a pre-game ritual or routine? A special place you watch sports events?

☞ Do you look forward and anticipate big events? What special plans do you make to ensure nothing interferes with you watching the event?

Reason #4–State Change

Fans experience physiological changes during a game. Male fans can experience a surge in testosterone after a victory and just as sharp a decline after a defeat. The Bleacherreport.com article coined the term "eustress," which is a combination of euphoria and stress. "Even among non-avid supporters, sport manages to bring about physiological changes, which induce various emotions like euphoria, dejection and stress."

Motivational self-help guru Tony Robbins calls these types of physiological changes a "state change." Robbins contends that to really change our behavior, we need a state change to snap us out of an old way of thinking and open us up to a new idea. He is an expert of creating an environment conducive to state change. That's why his seminars sell out all over the world and produce long lasting results.

We crave state change. That's why some people like to go to sad movies and have a good cry. Other people prefer to listen to loud rock music and scream along while others like to attend religious services that trigger intense inner reflection.

Whether it's music, movies, religion or sports, we use these mediums to help us produce a state change. We want to feel something differently than we currently feel and sometimes we use outside stimuli, like sports, to make that happen.

☞ If you are having a bad day, what activity produces a state change to help you feel better?

☞ How do sports produce a state change? How does the "thrill of victory or agony of defeat" help us feel differently than we did before we experienced it?

Reason #5—Sense of belonging

The most obvious reason sports fans endure savage heat, raging thunderstorms and blinding blizzards to watch their team is the sense of belonging to a larger group. The hottest I've been in my life was a late August, noon Gator football game in the Swamp (the University of Florida's football stadium), and I wouldn't have missed it for the world. There is no better feeling than sharing a game with 80,000+ like-minded screaming fans! At least we were all hot together!

Most sports teams have specific terminology for the collective group of fans further deepening the sense of belonging. Gator fans refer to themselves as the "Gator Nation" and, when we see a fellow fan wearing Gator gear, we greet each other with an enthusiastic "Go Gators!" Duke Basketball fans refer to themselves as the "Cameron Crazies" and have a series of cheers they chant in sync at the games. The Oakland Raiders fans, known as some of the rowdiest fans in the NFL, have a special section in the stadium labeled the "Black Hole." The fans in the Black Hole are known for dressing up in elaborate costumes and loudly voicing their opinion when a play is called in the opponent's favor.

Why do fans expend so much energy on a game? The sense of belonging to a larger group fills a primal need for connection. Sports fans feel like other fans are kindred spirits who understand and appreciate the same things they do. That common ground feels comforting in a distracted, popcorn-brain, highly-fragmented world.

In the BleacherReport.com article, one fan put it this way: "My ex-husband ran away with the lady next door, and I didn't seem to fit into suburbia anymore. The Knicks gave me purpose, something to do, a place to go. As a fan, I guess there is a sense of belonging. That you are a part of something." Well said!

☞ What is the name for the collective group of fans for your favorite sports team/individual?

_____

_____

_____

_____

☞ Why do you like being part of the group?

_____

_____

_____

_____

The more you become aware of your own fan behaviors, the better you will understand what your fans want. Start paying attention to your own fan related feelings, attitudes, beliefs and needs. This insight will pay huge dividends as you start to engage your fan base.

WHAT YOUR FANS WANT

So how do you engage your online audience? Tap into the DNA of a sports fan. If you know what appeals to an over-the-top sports fan, you know what will appeal to your customers.

Exact Target, a marketing software as a service company, recently released a research report titled "The Social Break-Up." They used extensive focus groups and online surveys to determine "why and how consumers engage with brands across the most popular interactive marketing channels, Facebook, email and Twitter."

The research concluded that a relationship with a brand begins with a "spark"—an initial decision to become "a fan, friend or follower" of a brand, which either progresses into a long-term relationship or ends in a nasty break-up, depending on how well the brand nurtures the relationship.

Email Marketing Do's & Don'ts:

☞ Do email relevant information to your audience. Segment your email lists into niched customer profiles and send only pertinent information to each segment.

☞ Don't email too frequently. Ask your fans how often they want to hear from you and respect their wishes.

☞ Do send out information only to people who ask for it. Build a permission based list of real fans.

☞ Don't build an email marketing list by buying names.

Facebook Do's & Don'ts:

☞ Do post valuable, informational posts on Facebook.

☞ Don't oversell with too many promotional messages.

☞ Do respect your fans' time. Over-posting on Facebook is a major turnoff.

☞ Don't forget to post consistently. Fans can forget about you if they don't hear from you regularly.

Twitter Do's & Don'ts:

☞ Do keep your tweets interesting. Twitter followers are less likely to break up with you if you regularly pique their interest.

☞ Don't bore your followers the same tweet over and over. They know it's pre-scheduled and not spontaneous.

☞ Do occasionally offer a special promotion to your followers as a thank-you for being a fan.

☞ Don't chit-chat about meaningless internal drama. Fans don't care about your problems.

Ultimately, your customers want to know you. Not the corporate identity, but the people and processes that make your company what it is. Fans want to peer behind the curtain and get a sense of what really goes on behind the scenes. When your clients feel like they know you, the real you, they can relate and identify with you. When a customer identifies with you they are yours for life!

Your customers want to feel good about themselves. Everyday life is overwhelming and exhausting. Your customers are looking for relationships that are like a Red Bull beverage: stimulating, positive and validating. These types of interactions feed the soul, replenish energy and keep us going.

Your fans want to escape the doldrums of everyday life. They look for relationships that add an element of fun, humor and lightheartedness to the mix. No one wants to do business with brands that add to their frustration and work load. Instead, clients want to escape through your products and services that transport them to a more relaxed, fun environment.

Your customers want to connect with you. They pay attention to communication that delivers an emotional message, especially ones that elevate their mood or trigger an insight and nostalgia. Engagement is all about the emotional connection.

Your clients want to belong. They want to feel part of something bigger. We as human beings crave that sense of belonging. It validates our existence. We feel okay because others like what we like. Even though our society is more connected than ever through technology, our basic human desire to belong to a group is stronger than ever.

FORMULATE YOUR GAME PLAN

Take time to answer the following:

1. Which aspect(s) of the DNA of a sports fan do you see in your fans?

_____

_____

_____

2. How can you use that insight to increase your sales?

_____

_____

_____

3. What changes do you need to make to your marketing (if any) to connect more to your fans?

_____

_____

_____

PART III

20 SLAM DUNK SECRETS

SECTION 1—IDENTITY

"Champions keep playing until they get it right."

Billie Jean King
Professional Tennis Player
12 Grand Slam Singles Titles,
16 Grand Slam Women's Doubles Titles &
11 Grand Slam Mixed Doubles Titles

PROFILE YOUR CUSTOMERS

The first secret to engaging your online audience is to truly know your customers. You need to know as much as possible about them if you want them to identify with your brand. You may think that "knowing your audience" sounds repetitive or old school, but the real impact to your bottom line is in taking action on this knowledge.

Answer these questions honestly:

- ☞ When was the last time you conducted a customer survey, focus group or one-on-one customer interviews?
- ☞ How often do you stop to compile customer feedback and analyze the data for big picture trends?
- ☞ Without your client list and project notes, could you give an accurate demographic and psychographic profile of your average customer?

We've all seen a television commercial and thought "that company doesn't get it" and wondered why the company pitched their product in that particular way. You've probably attended a social or business networking event and met someone who dominated the conversation and never asked about you. When these types of interactions occur we feel like the other person is talking "at" us and not "to" us. We feel like the other person or company doesn't care about us. No one wants to engage with someone or something that we can't identify with.

There are many helpful ways to learn about your customers including focus groups, surveys, salesperson feedback, website analytics, social media metrics and marketing research. Once you've pooled enough data for a reliable sample, use it to develop a customer profile.

Your customer profile should contain demographic details such as:

- ☞ Age
- ☞ Gender
- ☞ Ethnicity
- ☞ Household income
- ☞ Household size
- ☞ Occupation
- ☞ Location

Demographic data helps you select the right marketing avenues and platforms for your target audience. Internet marketing allows you to select which sites/pages your ads appear on based on detailed demographic and geographic data. It's both a smart and effective way to market to your audience.

In addition to collecting the demographic data, you should also learn more about the psychographic (buying motivations) characteristics of your customers. If you aren't familiar with psychographics, it is the study of psychological motivation as it relates to consumer buying behavior. The study of psychographics first began in the 1960s by Arnold Mitchell. His work led to the original VALS™ (Values and Lifestyles Study) model. In 1989, SRI International, Stanford University and the University of California, Berkeley, updated the model to reflect changing consumer behaviors. Today, the former Business Intelligence division of SRI International, known as the Strategic Business Insights (SBI), is the preeminent authority on VALS.™

The study of psychographics is "based on the premise that the mindset and demographics are more powerful than demographics alone." VALS uses psychology to describe the dynamics of underlying consumer preferences and choices. The VALS™ framework is comprised of three primary purchase motivations:

1. Ideals
2. Achievement
3. Self-expression

The VALS™ framework also measures a consumer's degree of resources, whether they have low resources, medium resources or high resources. According to VALS™ study, "Motivations and resources determine how a person will express himself or herself in the marketplace. People buy products and services and seek experiences that fulfill their characteristic preferences and give shape, substance and satisfaction to their lives."

Psychographics demonstrates that individuals with a high degree of "ideals" motivation typically buy what is "best" according to their values and beliefs, whereas individuals who are motivated by "achievement" buy products and services for social positioning. In contrast, those driven by "self-expression" buy products and services that allow them to truly express their personality and experience new adventures.

You can take a free quiz to determine your own purchase motivations at www.strategicbusinessinsights.com/VALS. You can also read more about the VALS™ on the Strategic Business Insights website and how to determine what types apply to your online clients.

The benefit of developing a customer profile is learning why your customers buy from you. If you can identify psychological purchase triggers it is much easier to produce engaging content that your clients will identify with.

One company that really taps into the buying motivation of their customers is TJ Maxx. This brand understands that their customer isn't the average bargain shopper who wants the lowest price; the TJ Maxx customer is a bargain shopper who wants to look fashion-forward on a budget. This subtle, yet important distinction in the buying motivation of their customers is very important. Shoppers who simply want clothing for the lowest price will shop solely on price at stores like Wal-Mart or K-mart. Shoppers who want a good price but also want trendy items will shop at stores like TJ Maxx or Target.

TJ Maxx's marketing tagline, "I'm a Maxxinista," is a play on the words "maximizing" and "fashionista," which speaks directly to the motivations of a TJ Maxx shopper. A good tagline like this one succinctly encapsulates the purchase motivations and helps current and potential customer identify with the brand.

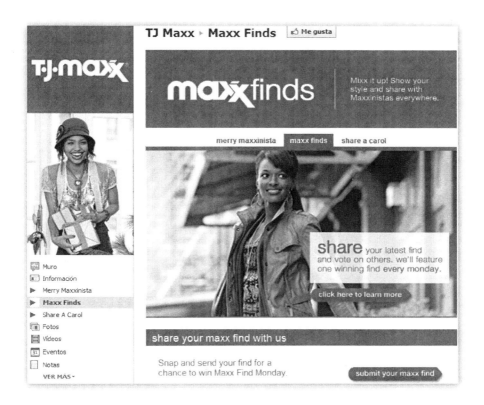

To create engagement that rises above the clutter and noise of traditional advertising, TJ Maxx took their marketing a step further with a weekly Facebook contest called "Maxx Find Monday." TJ Maxx Facebook fans submit a photo and a description of their latest bargain find from any TJ Maxx. The company narrows the weekly submissions down to the top three and then fans vote on the week's winner, who is featured on their Facebook Page. This contest is pure marketing genius!

TJ Maxx understands what motivates their shoppers: The thrill of the hunt for a good bargain. They also understand their shoppers love nothing more than showing off their latest finds. Contest entrants recruit their friends to vote for them, which also exposes TJ Maxx to a new group of potential customers. Meanwhile, TJ Maxx posts new merchandise on their Facebook Page to naturally continue the online conversation. "Maxx Find Monday" is a brilliant viral marketing campaign that proves TJ Maxx really knows their fans.

FORMULATE YOUR GAME PLAN

Take time to answer the following:

1. Create a customer profile:
   Age range _____
   Gender _____
   Ethnicity _____
   Household size _____
   Income Range _____
   Occupation _____
   Location _____

2. Complete this sentence, "My customers buy our products/services because…"

   _____

   _____

3. How does your product/service speak to each of the three buying motivations?
   Ideals _____
   Achievement _____
   Self-Expression _____

SHOW THE REAL YOU

How many glasses of wine are poured each year at the Epcot International Food & Wine Festival? 338,000!

Epcot is one of four theme parks on the Orlando Walt Disney World Resort campus. It features a World Showcase collection of pavilions that displays the culture of 11 countries. Every year from October through November, Epcot hosts a food and wine festival where visitors can sample the cuisine of each country. More than 160 renowned chefs serve more than 900,000 dishes and more than 100,000 miniature desserts. Paired with the delicious sample dishes are more than 338,000 glasses of wine and 750,000 cups of beer.

How do I know all of this? The Walt Disney Blog, of course. The blog has a great post on the Food & Wine Festival offering a look behind the scenes of this year's festival. I've attended this event many times (yum, yum!) and always wondered how Epcot pulls it off. Now I know!

The Disney Blog is an excellent example of how to help your customers identify with you. Show the real you!

Your customers easily tire of hearing the same corporate rhetoric and sales pitches. It's repetitive and boring. It's also what everyone else is doing. If this is what you offer, your message will blend into the background noise.

Instead give your customers what they crave—the inside scoop! Remember the marketing phrase for the National Enquirer tabloid, "Enquiring minds want to know." That phrase summarizes this secret perfectly. If you want to stand out in the marketplace, let your customers get to know you.

The blog post on the Food & Wine Festival stands out because it has a video featuring a cast member (Disney's term for employees) and her daughter as they tour the event. The video is very professionally done (of course, we expect nothing less from Disney), but also walks the fine line of being professional yet real and authentic. The script is conversational and feels like the narrators are talking right to you. They explain how the festival is planned and give tips just for viewers who plan to visit the event.

Nothing makes a customer want to listen to you and engage with you more than when they feel they know you. Disney does this better than any company because they consistently tell "The Disney Story" through marketing, merchandising and actions of their cast members. It is a full frontal brand assault every time you interact at any level with their brand.

You don't need to be as big as Disney to let your customers get to know the real you. And, this doesn't mean you have to give out personal details of your private life on Facebook.

"Real" content posting ideas:

- ☞ *Show behind the scenes of your operation.* How do you create your product/service? Who are the staff members behind your brand? What does it take to deliver your product/service on a daily basis?

- ☞ *Interview staff members on why they love your product/service.* Why do they work for you? What is their background? What are the challenges and surprises of their job?

- ☞ *Post about a special company events or community events that you participate in.* If you participate in any local charity events, talk about your participation and what it took to raise the funds or collect the goods you donated. Talk about causes or charities you care about and why they are important to your company.

Remember, when you show the "real" you, keep the message positive. You want to be authentic but don't drag your clients down with your daily frustrations. Think about it this way: Have you ever seen a piece of trash lying on the ground at Disney? No! Does trash exist at Walt Disney World? Of course. But the "real" Disney only goes so far. They share what is "real" as long as it stays congruent with the brand message.

In the world of corporate marketing, staying both true to your brand and positive is the correct approach. If you go too far with the "real" message, you may alienate segments of your customer base. Consider your brand message and your audience—and use the appropriate level of discretion. Of course, if your goal is to find a super-niched audience of people who appreciate an extreme perspective, then push the envelope in your degree of authenticity. As long as you know your customer, you will know how far to go.

FORMULATE YOUR GAME PLAN

Take time to answer the following:

1. What insights about your product/service or company would your customers find interesting?

_____

_____

_____

2. How do you plan to communicate that message?

_____

_____

_____

3. What action do you want a customer to take after learning more about the real you?

_____

_____

_____

WRITE LIKE YOU TALK

Thank you for your interest in our website. A representative will contact you within 24 hours. BLAH-BLAH-BLAH!

If you speak in corporate jargon, acronyms or flowery marketing language, your customers are going to tune you out.

Email programs aren't the only things with a spam filter. Today's consumer has a spam filter built right in and we know when we hear something belonging in the spam folder!

Whether you write copy for your website, post on Facebook or tweet on Twitter, you must write with a conversational tone that feels natural and sincere.

Which one of these posts is more conversational?

"Join us today for the Grand Opening of our new location on Main Street. Free food, music and games for the kids."

OR

"Will we see you today? Super excited for big Grand Opening event today on Main Street. Don't worry about your kids being bored, we have tons of games, food and music! See you there!"

All of your online copy should be as conversational as possible including:

- ☞ Website
- ☞ Blog
- ☞ Email
- ☞ Social media
- ☞ Videos
- ☞ Online ads

The secret to writing like you talk is to talk out loud as you type. Yes, your co-workers will think you are crazy (of course, they probably think that already), but it's worth it. As you compose copy, say it out loud. If what you've written doesn't flow naturally like you are having a conversation with another human being, then the copy is too stiff.

Keep in mind that for your corporate website, email campaigns and blog posts, you need to use correct grammar and punctuation. Keep it clean (some of you have a potty mouth out there). Check the spelling. No emoticons or text abbreviations like "LOL" please (except for tweets on Twitter because of the word limit). Strike the fine balance of conversing naturally while maintaining a professional tone. My basic rule of thumb is using language and tone that you would with a person you meet at a business networking event for the first time.

For a great example on how to write conversationally, check out the Starbucks Frappuccino Page on Facebook. Instead of posting stale, overly salesy posts about buying their tasty beverage, Starbucks posts about how to bake Frappuccino cupcakes and (extra points) the post was written by one of their fans! Awesome!

Another post features a picture of a Frappuccino clearly taken with a mobile phone (because it's not a perfect photo) captioned, *"Drinking Mint Mocha while playing Mint Mocha Challenge…things are getting pretty crazy around here."*

That post is very conversational, real and *engaging*. Customers wonder what the Mint Mocha Challenge is and how to get in the game.

Another Starbucks post summarizes exactly how their customers feel most days: *"It's Wednesday and needing a Frappuccino. That is all."* They could have written, "Stop by today and order a Frappuccino at your local Starbucks." Which one would you engage and identify with? Which one makes you want a Frappuccino more?

For your website copy and blogging, you may need to hire a professional writer to perfect your tone. I'll talk more about that later.

For your social media posts, it sounds more authentic and current if you do the posting for your company instead of outsourcing. A third party can learn your voice and post conversationally, but will take time and expertise. Hire carefully.

If you want to improve writing like you talk, ask a teenager. Tell them what you want to post and then ask them to "translate" for you. They can help you perfect your social media vernacular.

Start typing out loud as you type. It can transform your brand and engage your customers in a way you never thought possible.

FORMULATE YOUR GAME PLAN

Take time to answer the following:

1. On a scale of 1–10, how conversational is your online copy?

2. Which online site needs improvement first? Website, blog, email, Facebook or Twitter?

3. Do you need to hire a professional writer?

4. What is your first step to make your copy more conversational? When will you take that step?

BRAND YOUR SITES

Did you know someone buys a Burt's Bees Lip Balm every two seconds? Did you know that Burt's Bees donates 10 percent of online sales to The Greater Good Foundation? Did you know that for the past 25 years Burt's Bees has refrained from testing its products on animals?

If you don't know a lot about Burt's Bees personal care products for men and women, you can learn anything you want to know from their online presence. They tell the story of their all-natural, environmentally focused brand better than most companies. You may not purchase Burt's Bees products, but browsing their online marketing can help you improve yours.

One remarkable aspect of Burt's Bees online presence is how well they tell the brand story visually. In the last secret, we talked about writing conversationally and Burt's Bees does that exceptionally well. But they don't stop there. They also tell the story with visually compelling graphics consistent across all of their online sites.

☞ The online yellow, red, white and brown color scheme is consistent with the product merchandising and consistent across all sites, including the corporate website, product microsites, blog, email, YouTube, Twitter and Facebook Page.

☞ Burt's Bees uses the logo repeatedly in the graphics as a main graphic element, only changing it slightly depending on the use for each website. The result is a consistent look across all platforms.

☞ Burt's Bees Facebook Page has a customized profile image that matches the current graphic on the homepage of their corporate website. The Facebook Page also has a custom designed Welcome, Promotions and Coupon pages which complement the current creative on the corporate website.

☞ Burt's Bees Twitter and YouTube page profiles are customized to match the creative used on Facebook and the corporate website.

☞ Burt's Bees email campaigns continue the visual theme with complimentary colors and graphics.

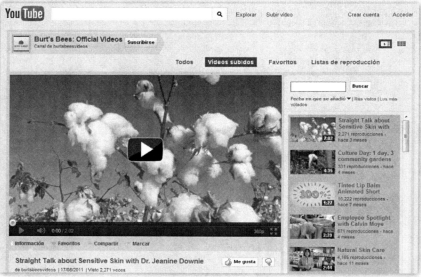

The good news for small and medium size businesses is that it's easier for them to achieve a consistent brand image than it is for larger companies. Imagine trying to coordinate all the aspects of an International brand involving multiple agencies, staff members, languages and cultures.

Because consumers are so distracted, you need consistent visuals to help them quickly identify your company. Companies like Nike and Target have perfected this approach with instantly recognizable logos. When you see a "swoosh" or a "bull's eye" graphic you instantly know it's a Nike or Target product. Target.com reports that "96 percent of people recognize the bulls eye, even edging out Nike and Apple." I want to know who the other 4 percent are and why the number isn't a 100 percent.

Consistent graphics provide a shortcut to busy customers who scan website pages quickly for information that interests them. Our eye is drawn to graphics and, specifically, graphics that don't look like a promotion.

Useit.com has a great case study in web design featuring the U.S. Census Bureau. They conducted a homepage usability test on www.census. gov. The test asked users to find the country's current population number. The answer was in the right hand side column in big red numbers. Unfortunately, 86 percent of users failed to identify the correct number. The researchers tracked the test subjects' eye movement on the page and found that while their eye saw the Population Clock the subjects didn't actually use it because it looked like an advertisement.[17]

The importance of compelling and consistent graphics cannot be overstated. You dramatically increase the chance of a fan engaging with your brand with a killer graphic presence consistent across all of your websites.

FORMULATE YOUR GAME PLAN

Take time to answer the following:

1. On a scale from 1–10, how consistent are your graphics across all of your online sites?

2. Do you have a customized Facebook Page, Twitter profile and YouTube Channel? If not, which one will you work on first?

3. Do you need to invest in creating meaningful graphics and images?

FEATURE YOUR FANS

A Microsoft fan named Brandon Foy recently landed the design job of his dreams with Microsoft. He did it by posting two homemade commercials on YouTube for the Windows phone. Both commercials have received hundreds of thousands of views. Microsoft leveraged the viral buzz by hiring Foy as a graphic designer. It's a win-win. Foy gets a job with a company he loves and Microsoft gets a passionate employee that is already recruiting new fans.

If you want your customers to identify with your brand, then feature real fans in your marketing. You don't have to go as far as Microsoft and hire them to work for you (although customers make great employees) but you can feature your fans and let them do the talking, which means you don't have to talk about yourself.

We naturally connect and respond to others that like what we like. It's high school all over again. We want to feel good about our purchase decisions and seeing others use a product/service gives us the validation we want and need. In fact, today's consumer cares more about what others say about your brand than what you have to say. In the age of websites like Angie's List and Amazon.com, user reviews can make or break a purchase decision. In a study performed by OTX Research, two-thirds of consumers use the information they find on social media to influence a buying decision. At least 67 percent are likely to pass this information on to others and 60 percent trust the information on social media more than they trust traditional advertising.

While you can't control user generated content like reviews and recommendations, you can proactively tell your story through the eyes of satisfied fans.

A good example of a campaign featuring fans is the "I'm Drinkin' Dunkin" campaign run by Dunkin Donuts in 2011. The campaign featured everyday Dunkin Donuts customers selected from an open casting call. The campaign spanned a number of marketing channels including television, radio, online marketing, social media, public relations and in-store promotional activities.

"We had more than 1,000 Dunkin' Donuts fans show up at the casting call, many were cast in the current commercials, including two firemen from Georgia," said Chris D'Amico, group creative director at Boston-based Hill Holliday, which created the campaign. "This campaign celebrates Dunkin' Donuts consumers and their love affair with Dunkin' coffee. It is also an invitation to try Dunkin' Donuts coffee."[18]

You can also feature your fans in your online marketing:

☞ *Use a different testimonial on each page of your website.* Don't relegate your testimonials to one page and hope your online visitors find it. Sprinkle them throughout the copy.

☞ *Capture testimonials in the moment on video with a point and share video camcorder or your smartphone.* Candid, real videos will receive more views on YouTube than overly produced, staged videos.

☞ *Conduct a fan centered contest on Facebook.* Allow fans to submit an entry such as a photo, video or poem incorporating your brand into the entry.

☞ *Invite fans to comment about your brand.* Take the time to thank them when you see a positive email, post or tweet.

☞ *Set aside a day for a photo shoot of fans using your product/service.* Make it fun and offer food and entertainment. Authentic photos of real fans are far better than stock photos.

☞ *Gather testimonials from all the departments in the company.* Post testimonials regularly on social media.

☞ *Hold a fan appreciation event.* Take lots of pictures and film it.

Fan marketing is not only effective, it's highly rewarding. It helps you remember why you work so hard in the first place. Keep in mind, without fans; you don't have a business to market.

FORMULATE YOUR GAME PLAN

Take time to answer the following:

1. How well do you consistently gather testimonials about your company? How can you go about collecting more?

_____

_____

_____

2. What do your fans consistently say about your business? What about it do they love?

_____

_____

_____

3. How can you repurpose fan testimonials across multiple sites?

_____

_____

_____

4. If you are not currently receiving spontaneous testimonials from fans, what can you do to encourage fans to do so?

_____

_____

_____

20 SLAM DUNK SECRETS

SECTION 2—SELF-ESTEEM

"A good coach will make his players see what they can be rather than what they are."

Ara Parashegian
Former Notre Dame Head Football Coach
1980 Inductee College Football Hall of Fame

BE A FAN OF YOUR FANS

I was working on a client project at my desk and stopped for a moment to check my Twitter stream on Hootsuite (a social media management dashboard tool). I was shocked and surprised to see that @CrystalLight (the official Twitter handle for Crystal Light beverages) had retweeted my post about how much I love their decaf lemon ice tea and had publicly thanked me for the tweet. I felt like a million bucks. A national brand had actually seen my tweet and personally responded. Wondering if it was a fluke, I started paying attention to Crystal Light on Twitter and have seen numerous similar tweets since. Genius!

Being a fan of your fans is a low-cost, easy way to build the self-esteem of your fans. Remember, your fans will engage with you more if your brand makes them feel good about themselves. Publicly acknowledging your fans is a great way to do just that.

You might wonder how Crystal Light knew I tweeted about them? Do you have to live at a computer 24/7/365 glued to Twitter in hopes of catching a positive mention? No!

Many social reputation management tools are available to monitor your social media mentions and will also alert you about whether those mentions are positive or negative. The sophistication of the tool needed depends on the size of your company and the amount of online marketing you use daily.

For small to medium size businesses, many free tools like Google Alerts and Social Mention will monitor a list of keywords and email you a notification any time they are used on the web or social media. I have Google Alerts set up for my name and my company name. I never tire of seeing what the other Meredith Olivers in the world are up to—sometimes it's bull riding in Spain or bungee jumping in Vegas! One thing's for sure, those Meredith Olivers are a lot more adventurous than I am!

Addict-O-Matic is another interesting online reputation management tool that monitors a particular keyword phrase and presents the latest buzz about the phrase across 18 sites from Twitter to YouTube in real time.

You should routinely type your brand name, product/service name and industry keywords into the search tool on Twitter and see what tweets come up referencing you. This practice gives you the opportunity to retweet and reply to fans who mention your brand. Social media dashboard tools like Hootsuite and Tweetdeck will automate the search process for you and present all of your mentions in a streaming column on their dashboard.

If you are a larger company, you may want a more robust monitoring tool like Shoutlet, Sprout Social or Alterian. These tools track your mentions and produce sophisticated reports about your social engagement levels.

Monitoring your positive mentions is important, and it's even more important if someone says something negative about your brand. We'll cover responding to negative comments in a later chapter. For now, let's focus on being fans of your fans by simply taking the time to personally respond when they mention how much they love your brand.

Another opportunity to become a fan of your fans is to reciprocate a follow or fan and become their fan in return. This is particularly effective with strategic business partners. In the world of fan marketing, it's important to give in order to receive.

- ☞ Proactively become a fan of your strategic partners' Facebook Pages.
- ☞ Sign up for a subscription to their blog and email newsletter.
- ☞ Freely write recommendations for them on LinkedIn.
- ☞ Find ways to publicly thank your strategic alliances for new business on your social sites.
- ☞ Proactively retweet their posts and thank them publicly when they do so for you.
- ☞ Welcome new followers on Twitter with a public welcome message and mention their twitter handle.
- ☞ Give a #FF (Friday Follow) shout-out on Twitter to fans that you follow and enjoy their posts. The Friday Follow tradition is a great way to acknowledge other Twitter users. Simply compose a post with the #FF hashtag and then list the Twitter handles of the fans you want to acknowledge.

One day I just know Jon Bon Jovi himself will personally write on my Facebook wall. When that day happens, I'm bronzing my computer monitor for all eternity!

FORMULATE YOUR GAME PLAN

Take time to answer the following:

1. Are you tracking mentions about your brand on the Web and social media?

2. Do you respond to positive mentions in real time with a thank you?

3. Do you need to set up social monitoring tools to help automate the process?

4. Who is the designated person on your team who responds to social media mentions and what is the response time goal?

BUILD A RELATIONSHIP

If you aren't sure how to maintain a positive relationship in the online world, think about what makes a good relationship in the offline world.

- Complete trust
- Open communication
- Mutual respect
- Quality time
- Thoughtful consideration
- Consistent commitment
- True loyalty

Positive relationships bring value to our lives and increase our self-esteem. You should maintain a relationship with your fans. I'm not talking about fans stalking you like the paparazzi everywhere you go, but a respectful, fun, social relationship that drives more sales.

In the B2B (Business to Business) sales arena, selling is all about relationships. The application of this time-tested secret is most easily seen in the B2B sales environment. But why don't we apply it to the B2C (Business to Consumer) sales arena? Many of you that sell directly to consumers are rolling your eyes right now and thinking, "I have to have a relationship on Facebook with these people? I don't even want to talk to my own family on Facebook, much less my customers!"

I get that kind of reaction all the time when I train sales people who sell to consumers. I frequently hear objections like, "I don't have time for social networking" or "I don't know how." It's interesting that we don't generally dispute the concept in the B2B world. B2B salespeople are expected to go above and beyond to build a relationship first and sell products/services second; for them, lack of time and desire is not an acceptable excuse.

The truth is, even in the B2C sales arena, lack of time can't be an acceptable excuse any longer either. Remember, old ways of marketing and selling no longer work. If they aren't working, you can't use them to grow your business. You have little choice but to "man up" and learn how to use social networking to build relationships with your fans. Who knows, in time you might enjoy it.

I confess I was one of the skeptics. I vividly remember a conversation with a fellow colleague where I told her salespeople would never use social networking and it should be relegated to the marketing department at the corporate level. She was very patient with me and has never come back to say "I told you so!" even though she has every right to do so.

If you are feeling overwhelmed, that's okay. I've felt that way too. All sales and marketing professionals have. There are so many tasks, not enough hands to do them and deadlines looming all around us. But, in our heart of hearts, that is why we are in the field—we thrive and enjoy the adrenalin rush of a lot of things happening at once. If this seems like too much with your current responsibilities, slow down for a moment. Take a deep breath and focus on one secret at a time. Keep your action steps simple and attainable. Set a goal to improve and then pick the book back up to work on the next secret.

Actions to help you build a solid relationship:

☞ *Post consistently.* Fans want to hear from you. Spend quality time "together" online.

☞ *Communicate openly.* If a fan posts something negative, don't delete the post and act like it never happened. Respond immediately with a next action step to investigate the complaint and work toward a resolution.

☞ *Follow through.* If you say you will post new pictures soon, stick to your word. If you promise a coupon is coming soon, make it happen. If you promise a resolution to a complaint, make sure the issue is resolved.

☞ *Observe netiquette.* Respect your fans privacy. Never, ever share their information with a third party no matter how much money you are offered.

☞ *Be authentic.* If your company doesn't really have a bounce house in the conference room, don't post that you do just to look more hip and trendy. Don't post fake testimonials and pose as customers.

☞ *Reciprocate kindness.* Do small things to thank your fans. Imagine how shocked a fan would be to receive a personal, hand-written thank you note from your CEO or a phone call from the chairman of the board. Don't forget about low-tech, high-touch acts that would mean a lot to someone.

☞ *Connect with fans.* If your fans have similar business interests, introduce them to each other (with permission, of course).

☞ *Offer value.* Don't make it all about you all the time. Post links and tips to help your fans save money and time or to improve the quality of their lives. We'll talk more about this in a later chapter.

Out of all of the online marketing options, a blog offers the best opportunity to develop a deeper relationship with your customers. It's hard to truly deliver valuable information in 140 characters or less. It's also hard to keep your corporate website up-to-date frequently enough to give out timely information. A blog allows you to share more in-depth information in the form of written, audio and video posts. You can categorize and tag posts to easily organize all of your content and keep it simple for customers to browse and interact with on your website. Invite blog readers to subscribe and comment on your posts.

My recommendation is to treat your blog as the hub of your online marketing strategy. I go into depth on this concept in *Click Power: The Proven System to Increase Sales.*

Post your core content on your blog and use other online sites to drive visitors to the blog. Think of your online marketing strategy like an old-fashioned wagon wheel with the blog at the hub of the wheel. The spokes of the wheel represent other sites that link to the hub like banner advertising, search engine optimization (SEO), paid search marketing, social media, email marketing and offline marketing like direct mail, signage, ads and brochures.

Good relationships evolve and change over time. The same is true with your fans. Some fans stay highly engaged for a while and then fade away. Others will begin to engage just as others fade. As long as you constantly nurture your fans, a pipeline of relationships will feed your sales goals for a long time to come.

FORMULATE YOUR GAME PLAN

Take time to answer the following:

1. How would you rate the strength of the relationships with your customers?

2. What is your social media policy? Do you have a written standard of what and who posts in your company?

3. How do you handle negative comments? What is your planned response time and follow-up process?

4. What three things could you start doing today to improve your online relationship with your customers?

REWARD LOYALTY

Nothing makes fans feel more loved than when you recognize and reward their patronage. A good reward program will provide value to members, give the business valuable feedback and increase repeat business, but if, and only if, the reward program is a good one.

If you currently run a reward program, does it really provide value to members? What is the quality of information you gain in return?

There are two basic types of reward programs:

1. *Free*—Your customer opts in with minimum information and the program is free to join. This can be effective, but doesn't really incentivize future purchases.
2. *Paid*—Your customer pays a fee to join the program. Even though customers are very cost conscious, many appreciate the exclusiv-

ity of a paid program as long as the value of the program is worth the fee. The value of a paid program can include future discounts, exclusive offers and upgraded service. A paid program will make your customers feel special and boost the link between self-esteem and your brand.

Online coupon giant Groupon recently launched a reward program for both its merchants and subscribers with a virtual punch card. Subscribers who purchase a Groupon offer receive additional discounts when they spend more than a dollar threshold with the merchant. The concept behind the program is to reward subscribers' loyalty to both Groupon and merchants by offering future discounts. The program also quiets Groupon critics who claim that Groupon doesn't deliver high quality customers.

If you already have a loyalty program, how well are you leveraging it in your online marketing?

- ☞ Information about the program should be easy to find on your corporate website.
- ☞ Your program should provide participants with the ability to refer others.
- ☞ Keep the sign-up form as short as possible while still gathering valuable data that you can use to refine your marketing strategy.
- ☞ Integrate the program into your Facebook Page and embed a sign-up form on the page so members can sign up immediately.
- ☞ Regularly communicate with your members via email (but don't overdo it) and offer value for the membership.
- ☞ Create a Twitter profile or use a specific #hashtag just for your reward members. Tweet exclusive information just for them.

☞ Promote the program on your blog. Regularly post about the benefits of the program and invite members to comment about how they've used their rewards.

Another option to reward fans' loyalty is by giving away free content just for fans. Create a special section on your website or blog just for current customers. If you want to make a stronger impression, create a separate fan website just for them. Provide them with login information or ask them to create a user profile. To learn more about this type of reward program, look at the entertainment industry. Radio stations, television programs and performing artists are very good at engaging fans with exclusive content. Sign up for your favorite band or artist's fan club and see first-hand how they engage their fan base.

Exclusive content posting ideas:

☞ Behind the scenes sneak peeks
☞ Early bird event and sale opportunities
☞ Exclusive photos and videos
☞ Interviews with company team members
☞ Fan-only contests and promotions
☞ Badges and widgets
☞ Fan-only merchandise

If you want to know the best way to reward your fans, ask them! Listen and pay attention to the comments. Who better to determine the direction of a loyalty program than the fans themselves?

FORMULATE YOUR GAME PLAN

Take time to answer the following:

1. Do you currently have a customer appreciation/loyalty program?

2. If no, what has stopped you? How can you overcome that obstacle moving forward?

3. Is your fan program easy to access and will it help users learn more about on all of your online sites?

4. How can you increase membership in your current program?

20 SLAM DUNK SECRETS

SECTION 3—ESCAPISM

*"I want to thank the Good Lord for
making me a Yankee."*

Joe DiMaggio
New York Yankee Professional Baseball Player
Three-time MVP, 13 Time All Star, 56 Game Hitting Streak

STOP SELLING

Your fans are already sold. That's why they chose to follow your blog and/or sign up for email updates. Maybe they haven't purchased yet, but they are at least sold on learning more about you. How long they remain sold is directly determined by what you do next.

Ever visit a company Facebook Page only to see post after post promoting a new product or service? How long did you stay a fan of the page? Probably not long.

Fans want to find solutions to their problems and escape the challenges of everyday life. Does your online marketing offer a safe haven where fans can receive authentic answers about the problems they dealing with?

The first step to developing a sound online strategy is determining what value you will provide your fans. This applies not only to your social media profiles, but also to your website and email content. What valuable insights will your fans care about?

Many business owners and sales people I consult with are very concerned that they don't have anything of value to say. This is a natural and common feeling. You probably don't think of yourself as an expert in your field, but the truth is, after you've worked in a particular position or industry for a reasonable length of time, you develop a specialized skill set that others will find valuable.

Tap into your knowledge base and turn the information into tips that your customers and strategic business partners can use. Zillow.com is a free real estate resource for home buyers, sellers, agents, mortgage professionals, insurance representative, home builders, and pretty much anyone interested in the buying or selling of residential real estate. Zillow's real estate database has more than 100 million U.S. real estate listings, including one-bedroom condos in Manhattan and celebrity mansions in Beverly Hills. Zillow could assume the extensive database of listings offers enough value to their website visitors, but they don't. The Zillow Blog acts as a comprehensive resource on all thing real estate. The blog offers helpful how-to tips on topics for consumers like "Four Real Estate Deal Killers" and topics for agents like "Agents Finding New Success with New Incentives." Zillow also offers light-hearted posts such as "What Do Celebrities Do in Those Glitzy Kitchens" and serious posts about the economy such as "30-Year Fixed Rate Rises Slightly, Remains at Historic Lows."

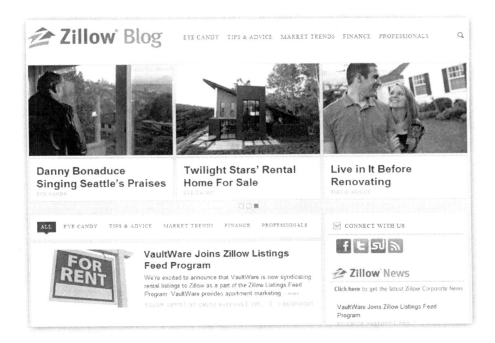

Zillow promotes its blog through posts on Facebook, Twitter, email campaigns and online advertising on other websites. The Zillow blog is an excellent example of how to take expertise and turn it into tangible value. Visitors repeatedly visit the blog to learn more, seek answers to questions and be entertained.

The blog also has a long online shelf life because industry professionals (non-Zillow employees) blog, tweet and post links to the Zillow blog posts. The high quality of the content keeps the posts evergreen and current to both new and old customers.

What does it take to create a blog with valuable content?

☞ *Brainstorm a list of frequently asked questions.* Write about what your customers and strategic business alliances frequently ask about. Content that answers frequently asked questions will be of interest to the audience and less self-promotional.

☞ *Plan an editorial schedule.* How often will you post? I recommend posting a new blog at least once a week. In some industries, where the audience is more tech savvy, you may need to post more often. How often to post comes back to knowing your fan profile.

☞ *Use a blogging platform that is intuitive to you.* I prefer the Wordpress platform but if you prefer Blogger or Typepad, that's okay, too. Pick whatever program is easiest for you.

☞ *Integrate your blog into your main website.* Gone are the days where the blog was a separate entity from your website. In some cases, the blog may actually become your main website. It all depends on your audience.

☞ *Brand your blog with complimentary graphics to your other sites.* We covered this in Secret #4. Go back and review that chapter if you have questions.

☞ *Categorize and tag your posts to easily find topics of interest.* Be selective when you categorize and don't create too many categories. You will dilute the effect.

☞ *Use graphics in blog posts to bring the copy to life.* A great photo or image can translate to as much value as a 760-word post. Blog readers generally look at pictures and headlines first and your copy second.

☞ *Link to other resources.* Embed links in your posts to other sites that offer valuable information and include a "blog roll" (list of recommended links) in the sidebar of your blog.

Delivering value as a selling tool is as much attitude and state of mind as it is a marketing technique. You can train your mind to become more aware of possible post topics. Content is everywhere around you from everyday interactions with others to lessons learned on the job. When you have a brainstorm for a new post topic, make sure you write it down or better yet, record a memo on your smartphone and email it to yourself. You can even use a free app called Dragon to record a memo and have it automatically converted into a text document. Whether you go low-tech or high-tech, get in the habit of recording your ideas before you forget them.

FORMULATE YOUR GAME PLAN

Take time to answer the following:

1. Make a list of the top 10 most frequently asked questions by your customers and strategic business partners.

2. Could you write approximately 300–350 words (approximately 10–12 sentences) on each question? Congrats, you are a blogger!

3. If you answered no to #2, or don't have the time, how are you going to make a blog happen?

4. From a technical perspective, what are your next steps to starting a blog?

WHEN YOUR FANS PLAY, THEY PAY

One of my favorite Facebook promotions of all time is the recent Bush Beans "Make Me An Offer" promotion. You may be familiar with Bush's Beans from their clever television commercials with the talking dog who claims to know the secret Bush family bean recipe.

The "Make Me An Offer" promotion on Facebook invites fans to make Duke (the company mascot) an offer in exchange for the secret family recipe. Thousands of fans wrote in with clever quips and Duke quickly responded to every one of them. The banter between the page and the fans was hilarious and absolutely engaging—so much so I personally found it distracting to stay focused on my computer work. I wanted to stay on the page to see what Duke was going to stay next. And, the next time I went to the grocery store, I picked up a couple of cans of Bush's Baked Beans. The brand was on the top of my mind as I strolled down the canned vegetable aisle (and they are really tasty!).

Many factors made this a great campaign. Bush's Baked Beans integrated their television commercials into their social media presences. The campaign was fun and certainly provided an escape to fans. The campaign was also interactive and asked fans to get involved.

Best Buy and Brookstone outsell their competitors for many reasons, one of those reasons is that when consumers play, they pay. How many times have you picked up an item in Brookstone at the mall intending just to kill time while you wait on someone else to finish up their shopping and ended up buying it? You had no intention of purchasing the item, but after you played with it, you couldn't imagine leaving it at the store. I happen to own a very expensive iJoy massage chair for this very reason! In the online world, customers do not physically pick up your product, so we need to find other ways to increase interactions.

Another great Facebook Page that encourages fan interaction with the brand is the Oreo Cookie Page. To celebrate Oreo cookies new availability in Germany, Oreo launched an interactive Facebook contest where fans could submit a video to "Help Helmut" (a fictional German character) understand how to enjoy an Oreo cookie. An app guides fans through the video creation. The three top videos (decided by Helmut) are awarded the coveted look-alike Gartzenburg (which appears to be a Travelocity-like gnome statue). The video submissions are absolutely hilarious and certainly provide an escape to the fans.

If you conduct any contest on Facebook specifically, make sure you adhere to the Facebook Fan Page Promotion Guidelines. You can learn more about those guidelines by clicking on the Terms link at the bottom of your Facebook Page. If you don't adhere to the rules, you risk having your page shut down by Facebook and wasting all of your hard work building a relationship with your fans.

It's easy to spot good interactive content, but more difficult to develop your own since you are so close to your brand. The more you solicit feedback from your fans and the more you know your customer profiles, the easier it is to brainstorm fun content they will enjoy and engage with regularly.

If you are trying to come up with a contest idea, ask the following questions:

- ☞ What action words describe how customers use our product/service?
- ☞ Is the product/service delivered in an interesting way?
- ☞ When and where is our product/service used?
- ☞ How often do your customers use it?

☞ Is there anything funny or quirky (keep it clean and politically correct) about your product/service?

☞ Are there any minor challenges (nothing so serious that would prevent someone from using the product/service) that are humorous?

☞ What are the universal challenges your target audience faces every day that you can turn into an interactive experience?

If you imagine yourself as the customer, you can probably come up with a clever premise for an interactive campaign theme. If not, leave the creative ideas to the professionals and hire a marketing company to come up with the concept and design the creative. If you do outsource, make sure the marketing company's ideas are congruent with your brand and will feel authentic to your fans.

FORMULATE YOUR GAME PLAN

Take time to answer the following:

1. What type of user generated content would your fans be likely to enjoy submitting? Photos, videos, poems, songs, drawings?

2. If you run an interactive campaign, what is its purpose ? What do you hope to gain from it?

3. How will you measure the success of the campaign?

4. Are in your compliance with the Facebook Fan Page Promotion Guidelines?

ANGRY BIRDS ANYONE?

I recently saw a vintage Atari "Flashback 3, Classic Game Console" for sale at Rite Aid. It was $39.99 and came with three games, including the uber-popular Asteroid. I guess if you wait around long enough, anything can come back into style. I can't imagine paying $39.99 for an Atari that uses decades old technology, but then I've never been much of a video gamer (even when I had the original Atari back in the day!). Even so, I'm sure there are enough nostalgia buffs to make this a profitable product.

If you aren't a gamer, it's easy to dismiss the validity of using online games as part of your fan engagement strategy. A look at the numbers should make you reconsider. According to Gartner, Inc., a leading information technology and research firm:

☞ By 2015, more than 50 percent of organizations that manage innovation processes will gamify those processes.

☞ By 2014, a gamified service for consumer goods marketing and customer retention will become as important as Facebook, eBay or Amazon.

☞ More than 70 percent of Global 2000 organizations will use one gamified application.

Research aggregator eMarketer reports that in 2011 U.S. gamers will spark $653 million in revenue solely from purchasing virtual items. That figure is expected to reach $792 million in 2012.

What does it mean to "gamify" something? "Gamifying" is the process of using game techniques and applying them to non-game scenarios. Essentially it means to make something fun! When you gamify your business, you give your fans the opportunity collect, win or earn virtual goods like:

☞ Badges
☞ Points
☞ Levels
☞ Leaderboards
☞ Challenges

Many software platforms can administer and manage your online game, such as Badegeville, BigDoor and Bunchball.

Games are particularly effective with Generation Y consumers. They expect to have fun and compete with each other for prizes.

An example of successful gamification is Foursquare. They successfully engage consumers by awarding badges to users. Every time you check in to a physical location on Foursquare you receive points. Points add up to unlock badges and titles. First time users receive "Newbie" badges and repeat visitors to a location can claim the title of "Mayor." The more you check in at a location, the more points and badges you earn. Friends compete against each other to oust the current mayor and become the new mayor. What a powerful third party endorsement of the brand!

If this seems foreign to you, remember it's really all about having fun. That's it. Your fans want an escape from the stress of life and you provide that in an interactive way while promoting your brand at the same time. It's a win-win.

FORMULATE YOUR GAME PLAN

Take time to answer the following:

1. How could gamification be part of your online marketing strategy?

2. Do you have an offline rewards or points system that you could easily gamify in the online world?

3. What steps do you need to take to implement a game into your marketing? When would you take the first step?

THE EASY BUTTON

I love the Staples Easy Button. It is one of my favorite advertising campaigns of all time. The television commercials are so effective that Staples actually made an Easy Button for their fans. I bought one for my desk. I use it as a reminder to keep things easy for our clients.

Making engagement easy is critical to engaging fans and attracting new fans. No matter how much your fans love and support your business, they are busy with their own day-to-day lives. The easier you make it for people to interact with you and your content, the more engagement you will receive from your fans.

Add links to your social media profiles on your website, blog and email signature.. Position the links prominently and be consistent with the placement from page to page. Cross-promoting your social sites is the best way to synergize your efforts and increase your fan base.

If you post consistently on social sites, add a live feed of your posts to your website or blog. This extra step gives website visitors the opportunity to easily see the quality of your posts and become a fan. Facebook provides several social plugin options for your website or blog. You can learn more about them at http://developers.facebook.com/docs/plugins/. Options include:

- *Like Button*—Visitors can share content from your site on their Facebook profile with one click.
- *Send Button*—Visitors can send your content to their friends.
- Subscribe Button—Visitors can subscribe to other Facebook users from your site.
- *Comments*—Visitors can comment on your content.
- *Activity Feed*—Visitors can see other fans' likes and comments.
- *Recommendations*—Visitors receive personalized recommendations about parts of your site they might like.
- *Like Box*—Visitors can like your Facebook page from your website.
- *Login Button*—Visitors can log in to Facebook from your website.
- *Registration*—Visitors can register on your website using their Facebook log-in information.
- *Facepile*—Displays the Facebook profile pictures of other fans and their activity on your site.
- *Live Stream*—Allows visitors to share activity and comments in real time during a live event.

Facebook social plug-ins offer many ways to customize your website. Twitter, YouTube and LinkedIn also offer social plug-in options. An important caveat, however: Limit the number of social plug-ins you add to your website to two or three or it will become overwhelming and distracting to your visitors. Select the plug-in that most accomplishes your online marketing and sales goals.

Another easy and affordable way to encourage fan participation is through social sharing buttons. Sites like ShareThis.com and AddThis.com offer social sharing button plug-ins for free. These free sharing buttons allow website visitors to share your content with others. Prior to the plug-ins, visitors had to be savvy enough to copy your website's URL and paste it into an email or social media post. With the plug-in, it has become one click easy to share your content right from your site.

Most of the social sharing plug-ins offer a non-registered version and a registered version. I recommend the registered version so you can track your social sharing activity. Most sharing plug-ins also integrate with Google Analytics reporting.

You can custom configure the sharing toolbar with the social sites of your choice. I recommend at least including Facebook, Twitter, Google+ and email. You might also want to include the print button in your toolbar.

Remember, if you add any of the plug-ins that allow for comments, you need to be monitor and respond to those comments. Don't leave your fans hanging. Acknowledge all comments, good or bad.

If you add a feed to your website or blog, you may also want to add a Twitter feed to your Facebook Business Page. Several apps are available to customize your Facebook Page and will feed in your LinkedIn, YouTube and Twitter activity to Facebook. The likelihood of someone seeing your content from other social sites increases dramatically if they see it on the site they are currently visiting. If this seems redundant, it is. One-click easy is the key. You want to make accessing your entire online marketing one-click easy from whatever page your fans are currently visiting.

FORMULATE YOUR GAME PLAN

Take time to answer the following:

1. On a scale of 1 to 5 (1 being lowest), how easy is it for website visitors to access your blog and social media profiles?

2. What tools are you currently using to encourage social sharing of your content?

3. What could you do to encourage your fans to share your content more often?

20 SLAM DUNK SECRETS

SECTION 4—STATE CHANGE

"Pain is temporary. Quitting lasts forever."

Lance Armstrong
Professional Cyclist
7 Time Consecutive Tour de France Winner

TIME YOUR MESSAGES

If you are going to post online content, make sure you post at optimal times so your target audience will see the post. Posting an obligatory message every morning at 8:15 so you can check it off the list isn't necessarily going to maximize engagement with your fans. Nor will it surprise and delight your fans enough to cause a state change.

"Twitter is reporting more than 200 million tweets per day and, according to its calculations, a day's worth of tweets would be enough to write a 10-million-page book or 8,163 copies of *War and Peace*. Every second, 2,400 tweets are sent through Twitter's servers, enough for 1.4 billion tweets per week." according to Mashable.[19]

WOW! Don't be discouraged by this statistic, just know for maximum impact you want to time the release of your posts to coincide with most users surfing habits. When should you post for the best results? Dan Za-

rella, social media scientist at Hubspot, has studied the best times to tweet on Twitter and post on Facebook. Here are some of his recommendations:

1. If you want your content shared on Twitter in the form of retweets, post at 5 p.m.
2. The best days to tweet are generally midweek and on the weekends.
3. The best time of day to encourage clicks on links included in your tweets is noon (lunch time) and 6 p.m. (after people arrive home from work).
4. The best day for sharing on Facebook is Saturday at noon and a little after 7 p.m.

However, Saturday is not necessarily the best day for posting for every industry. BuddyMedia did its own study and found that engagement on Facebook posts peaks on Thursday and Friday. That coincides with Facebook's own study that its "Happiness Index"—which measures the positivity of users' posts—rises by 10 percent on Friday. The company also found that shorter posts, or those with 80 characters or less, have a 27 percent higher engagement rate. BuddyMedia's study also found that brands posting outside of business hours (early in the morning, at the end of the work day and late at night) had a 20 percent higher engagement rate.

How do you know what works for your audience? Ask them. Also vary your posting times and pay attention to times of day and days of the week when you receive the highest amount of engagement.

Reviewing your online metric reports can provide valuable feedback. Google Analytics is a free, easy-to-use reporting tool for websites and blogs. Use it to learn about website visitor behavior trends. Information about Top Content Visited and Goal Conversions Percentages help you tweak your website navigation to place the most popular content in your primary navigation. Google Analytics can guide you through posting the types of content your audience values and engages with.

Facebook's Insights Report also offers helpful feedback on engagement trends. You can embed Google Analytics on your social media sites as well to track further engagements. Social media dashboard software tools like Hootsuite also offer reports that will show you when your fans tend to engage with your content, what type of content they click on most often and what sites the clicks originate from. If you are willing to pay for custom reports, Hootsuite offers advanced reporting options too.

FORMULATE YOUR GAME PLAN

Take time to answer the following:

1. Do you vary the timing of your social media posts?

_____

_____

_____

2. Are you consistently reviewing your analytics reports for trends?

_____

_____

_____

3. If you aren't receiving a lot of "likes," comments or retweets, how can varying the timing of your posts help improve engagement?

_____

_____

_____

LIGHTEN UP

Most of us take our work way too seriously. Unless you really are a neurosurgeon, most jobs are not brain surgery and people don't live or die based on the quality of our work. For those whose work is life or death, such as health care workers, military service members and law enforcement agents, you are our heroes!

When appropriate, lighten up about your work and life in general. **Fans respond when your content causes a state change and humor usually engenders loyalty.** However, be cautious that your humor doesn't alienate or make fun of your fan base in a negative way. Keep your humor clean and politically correct (unless your brand is purposefully not politically correct).

One of the safest forms of humor for business is what I call "Jerry Seinfeld" humor—observations about the quirks of everyday life. This type of humor is easy for most people to relate to and produces many comments among your fans.

Do you remember the classic Seinfeld episode where the rental car company lost Jerry's reservation? He stood at the car rental counter and said, "…The key to a reservation is to hold the reservation…" It is an easy laugh because everyone relates to a frustrating travel situation where our reservation wasn't handled as expected.

Observational humor requires an awareness of what's happening around you. It doesn't hurt to have a smartphone or tablet to capture the moment in the form of a photo or video. Then, you can post a graphic image, which is more impactful than a plain text post.

If something in everyday life causes you to stop, scratch your head, and then chuckle, chances are your fans will find it funny too.

You may remember when a venomous adolescent Egyptian cobra went missing from its enclosure at the Bronx Zoo. Within hours of the news media reporting the escape, someone created a Twitter parody profile @ BronxZoosCobra and began narrating the escapades of the missing animal. It was absolutely hilarious and went viral on Twitter in a matter of hours. Bottom line, it was fun and definitely caused a state change in the middle of a hectic, stressful day. **Sometimes you need to give your fans pure fun.** No hidden agenda, no bigger picture, just light-hearted, non-business related fun.

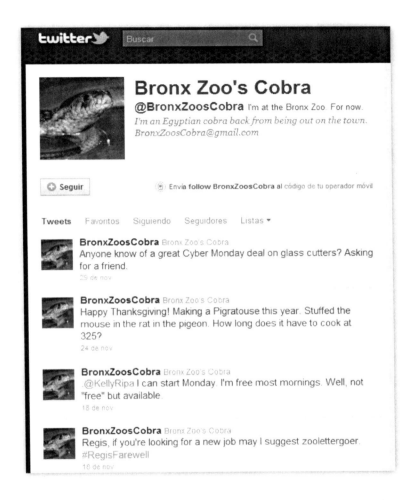

TMG's blog, Engage, summarized perfectly what we can learn from the Bronx Zoo Cobra: "People identify with themselves as a consumer first, regardless of their occupation. Acknowledging that can only help your social media efforts. Even if the subject matter of your industry is somewhat dry, you can use social media to spice things up a bit and relate to your audience as the movie-watching, iPod-listening, sit-com-laughing people they are."[20]

FORMULATE YOUR GAME PLAN

Take time to answer the following:

1. How often do you use humor in your marketing? Do you need to use it more or less?

_____

_____

_____

2. Is your humor appropriate to your target audience? How do you know?

_____

_____

_____

3. How can you take advantage of humorous situations in everyday life and convert them into marketing opportunities?

_____

_____

_____

KEEP IT FRESH

You won't truly impact your fans and produce a state change with stale content. **You need a content development and posting strategy.**

- ☞ How often do you plan to post new content?
- ☞ Who will develop the new content?
- ☞ How will you ensure the content is integrated with your other marketing efforts?
- ☞ What is the purpose of the content? How does it fit into your brand story?
- ☞ How will you ensure your content is properly optimized for search engines and fits within your overall search engine marketing strategy?

These are important questions. Don't be concerned if you don't know the answers right now. Let's take one at the time and work our way through them.

How often should you post new content?

The answer depends on your audience and the platform. Audiences of entertainment brands tolerate more frequent posts than corporate-type brands. As a general rule, here are a few posting guidelines per platform:

Corporate website

Refresh content monthly for non-ecommerce sites and weekly for ecommerce sites. Focus on adding new product/service photography/images, refreshing product descriptions and adding new testimonials.

Blog

Post a new blog at least once a week. The more frequently you post on a blog, the faster your audience will grow. If you can post several times a week your blog audience will grow faster. Don't be discouraged if no one comments or subscribes to the blog at first. Keep at it. If you produce high quality content frequently enough and promote the content on multiple sites, your readership will build.

Facebook

Post several times a week, but no more than a couple times a day. Again, you have to know your target audience. The more conservative the audience, the more likely you will annoy them with over posting. However, if you under post, you will lose your audience as well. The best way to strike a balance is to review your Facebook Insights reports. If you steadily gain new "Likes" for your page, then you've hit the right balance. If and when your page sees an increase in "Unlikes," then you are over posting.

Twitter

Post a few times per day. This is where I typically get the most resistance in terms of time management. Again, using a social media dashboard service and your smartphone can really make this easy to do. You can pre-schedule your posts, which helps manage your daily posts. However, don't overuse these tools because they take the spontaneity out of Twitter.

YouTube

Post new videos as needed. If you receive a great fan testimonial, post it. Have a new product? Create a video for it. Want to give out tips on how to use one of your products/services or a related product/service? Record a video. Remember that Generation Y, also known as the Millennials, are more likely to watch a video about your brand than read any text.

Email Marketing

Send an eNewsletter email campaign once a month, or at most, twice a month. Send promotional emails (eBlast or eFlyer) no more than twice a month. Add up all the types of emails you send (minus the transactional email regarding account balance, activity, rewards, etc.) and don't send more than one per week. In fact, I believe that weekly emails are still too frequent and wear out your email list. I would try to keep your email totals to around three per month. Certainly send no more than one email per week to your audience.

What content are you going to post?

You want to post a blend of valuable information, purely fun content meant to entertain, social information that connects fans together, news items to inform and community/local area information to connect your brand to a bigger purpose. **The key is to think like a journalist.** Much of this content exists everywhere around you. You have to learn how to capture it in the moment and repurpose it for your brand. Having the right smartphone is essential. I prefer the iPhone because of the number of apps available and the ease of use. Regardless of the type of smartphone you choose, invest time in learning how to use it. Always take full advantage of your phone's functionality.

Thinking like a journalist means actively looking for content ideas in your daily work and seizing the moment to snap a quick picture, record a video, send a tweet or update the company status.

This type of content creation works great for social networking sites. Blog, corporate website and email content creation will take more planning. Coordinate content so it all works together to subtly promote your brand. Map out an editorial schedule of your blog posts so you can plan a content theme and create a series of posts on a particular topic. Make use of guest contributors to your blog. Invite your strategic business alliances to post on your blog. Guest posts fill in content when you are busy, on vacation or have writer's block. Just make sure whatever your guests contribute is educational and not an overt sales pitch.

You can also repost other blog posts on your blog if you obtain permission from the author, give full credit and link to the original blog. Don't post content found on paid membership only sites. Keep in mind that reposting content from other sources is not always the best way to connect to your audience. Most of your blog content should be original to show your readers who you are and what your company is all about. The best practice, if you want to repost another blog, is to paraphrase the other blog and link to it. Consult your intellectual property attorney for details on what is and is not allowed in this area. Never plagiarize blog content.

Andy Beal, CEO of Trackur, posted a terrific article on the American Express Open Forum, titled "The 4-Hour Social Media Workweek"[21] and talks about the challenges of fitting social networking into an already over-scheduled work week. He recommends the following formula:

☞ *10 minutes a day for listening*—Spend 10 minutes a day monitoring what others say about your brand.

☞ *15 minutes a day for responding*—Spend 15 minutes a day replying to tweets, blog comments and email responses.

☞ *10 minutes a day for sharing*—Beal advocates picking one thing per day to share with your fans.

☞ *10 minutes a day for creating*—Write a few sentences per day and by the end of the week, you will have a new blog post.

That's 45 minutes per day divided into small segments. **I guarantee there are 10-minute time-wasters throughout your day that could be eliminated.** What marketing activities are you doing right now that could be automated, delegated or eliminated (because they no longer work)? Those extra minutes would give you the time needed to engage your fans. Find the time. Your future sales depend on it!

If this still seems overwhelming to you, then outsource content creation. You can effectively outsource website updates, blogging and email marketing. You can outsource social media posts too, but they are generally more effective done in-house. Creating your own social media posts that are done in real time means you'll come across as more authentic than if you use an outsider whose work you'll have to approve before posting.

FORMULATE YOUR GAME PLAN

Take time to answer the following:

1. List the sites you will post content on?

_____

_____

_____

2. Write down the frequency per site you plan to post.

_____

_____

_____

3. Is there an overall content theme that will help you select topics and brainstorm posting ideas?

_____

_____

_____

I DID IT MY WAY

know my husband's Starbucks order by heart. Venti, vanilla iced latte, no whip, Splenda®. At first remembering the order was as confusing as memorizing the secret codes to the "red button" at the White House, but in time I memorized it and most of the time get it right.

Companies like Starbucks and Burger King (which was a pioneer with its "Have it your way" campaign years ago) have trained consumers to expect customization even on the most inexpensive items. Today successful brands offer customers an array of packages to choose from and the ability to create their own package of products/services.

The Millennials are particularly keen on customization. In "American Millennials: The Choice Generation," Gigi Carroll, vice president and creative strategist at Draftfcb, observes: "Millennials crave customization, whether it's a t-shirt, a ringtone, a Facebook page, YouTube, or American

Idol."[22] The Millennial generation has grown up in a world where everything from mobile phone cases to M & Ms are totally customizable.

In addition to customization, consumers increasingly want DIY (do-it-yourself) products/services. Alexander Chernev, an associate professor of marketing at Northwestern's Kellogg School of Management, calls it "The Ikea Effect," which is not only the desire to customize products but also to participate in the creation process. Chernev notes "customers derive additional value in doing something themselves." Customers who purchase furniture at Ikea not only get to select from a variety of components to furnish a space, they get to assemble the furniture themselves. It's a win-win! Affordable, stylish and unique, every Ikea room is a one-of-a-kind. That speaks directly to the heart of a Millennial consumer.

You can capitalize on the customization expectation and the DIY desire by offering your fans a custom experience on your website. Consider adding a fan only section to your website where fans can login, create a profile, customize the profile, download badges and wallpaper to their computer. Google does a terrific job of offering custom choices to its account holders. Users can customize their Gmail interface not only in terms of functionality but design and style as well.

Another option is to allow fans to create a customized, digital version of your product/service on your website. For example, at Ford.com, Mustang fans can custom build their very own digital Mustang right down to the door handles. The digital creations are entered into a contest where creators battle it out for votes on Facebook and the Mustang website. Customers interested in purchasing their creation can see a local Ford dealership about pricing and details. This type of fan engagement capitalizes perfectly on the trend of customization and DIY personalization.

Creating an app for your business is another great way to customize your fans experience. In its article, "The Web is Dead. Long Live the Internet," Wired Magazine predicted that the Web will eventually become obsolete because we will use apps exclusively to conduct online activities.[23] Why? Because apps are specific and have limited functionality so they are quicker and more efficient than a blanket Google search that make take several tries to get to the right information.

For example, want to know something as specific as where in a movie is the right place to go to the bathroom? There's an app for that! It's called RunPee. No kidding! The app tells you the slowest part of the movie and will give you the transcript of the dialogue while you are in the restroom so you don't miss anything. There are hundreds of thousands of apps available that can solve any problem, find any piece of information or simply provide entertainment during down-time.

Creating an app for your business allows your repeat customers the ability to utilize core online functionality in a much simpler, user-friendly way than your website does. Your fans will appreciate the ability to customize their fan experience.

Remember that anything that is clickable is trackable. You can monitor all of this fan activity and use it for research and development of new products and services. And, who knows, maybe a fan will create a custom version of your product better than what you currently offer and be the million dollar idea you've been searching for.

As they say on American Idol, "Yo dawg, you really made that song your own."

FORMULATE YOUR GAME PLAN

Take time to answer the following:

1. If you are a smartphone or tablet user, think about your favorite apps. What problem does the app solve?

_____

_____

_____

2. What common problem do your fans share? How does your product or service solve that problem?

_____

_____

_____

3. How could you use technology like an app or customized fan page on your website to help fans solve their problems?

_____

_____

_____

20 SLAM DUNK SECRETS

SECTION 5—SENSE OF BELONGING

"Ask not what your teammates can do for you.
Ask what you can do for your teammates."

Magic Johnson
Retired NBA Professional Basketball Player
3 NBA MVP Awards, 9 NBA Final Appearances, 12 All Star
Games & 4 NBA Championships

GET INVOLVED

A great way to engage your current fan base and reach new fans is to promote and contribute to social causes. Not only will your business benefit, but you can give back and help those who are less fortunate. For a good example of how a powerful social media presence can raise awareness and interest in a cause, look no further than international pop icon Lady Gaga. She is the first female artist in history to claim five #1 hits from a debut album and the only artist in the digital era to top the 5 million sales mark with her first two hits.[24]

Love her or hate her, Lady Gaga is a social media maven. According to CelebGuru.com, Lady Gaga is the second most popular celebrity on Facebook (Eminem is number one) with 32,000,000+ fans, and the most popular celebrity on Twitter, with 16,000,000+ followers. She posts frequently and uses the tools to give back to her fans she has nicknamed "little monsters."

Her fans are rabid supporters who feel a deep connection to the singer through her devotion to them.

In a recent interview on the Ellen DeGeneres Show, Lady Gaga told Ellen that her newest photo book was created solely for the fans as a thank you for their loyalty. She is quoted many times saying she does everything for her fans, including naming her tour, "The Monster Ball," in their honor. Most artists take a year or two between tours to rest and recuperate, but she is hitting the road again, immediately following her last tour, because she loves to be with and perform for her fans.

In February 2011, Lady Gaga signed on as the spokesperson for the MAC AIDS fund, the philanthropic arm of MAC Cosmetics. MAC's cosmetic line, VIVA GLAM, donates all proceeds to the fund. Her involvement raised $34 million in one year—more than VIVA GLAM raised in total in the first 10 years of its inception.[25]

How did Lade Gaga do it? It wasn't an overnight process. During the past several years she built an incredibly engaged fan base. Her fans feel she is authentic and really cares about their daily lives. When she asks them to support a cause, they do it. It's that simple and complex at the same time. One morning she tweeted, "I am VIVA GLAM today. I'll be on GOOD MORNING AMERICA at 8:05 to talk about safe sex, glamour, and being Born This Way!"

MAC is thrilled with the results and made a strong social media presence a requirement for the next VIVA GLAM spokesperson.

What can you learn from Lady Gaga?

☞ *True fan engagement doesn't happen overnight.* You have to prove to your fans that you really care about them. That takes time. It's like any relationship. You must cultivate and invest in it. The best relationships are two-way equal partnerships where both parties feel like they are benefiting.

☞ *Once you have a loyal fan base, you can ask them to support causes you believe in.* Fans respect organizations that have a bigger mission and purpose beyond bottom line profits.

The social cause you support should align with your brand and further your brand story. The VIVA GLAM cosmetic line is a good example of how MAC married its core competency of high-end studio quality cosmetics with a pop icon likely to wear and appreciate their products.

After you've selected a cause to support, plan how you will engage your fan base. It could be as simple as donating a dollar for every new Facebook Page "Like" to the cause of your choice or a social media contest soliciting fan generated content such as photos and videos about the cause.

This strategy isn't limited to social causes. It also applies to trade associations and partner organizations you belong to. Promoting trade associations strengthens your reputation in the industry and increases employee loyalty as well as strengthening new talent recruiting efforts.

Your fans don't want to hear only about you all the time. To watch your engagement soar, tap into social causes and industry groups that your fans care about.

FORMULATE YOUR GAME PLAN

Take time to answer the following:

1. Does your organization support a social or local cause?

2. If yes, how can you incorporate online tools to help support and promote your efforts?

3. What are the benefits of supporting a social cause to your organization?

CELEBRATE TOGETHER

Avid sports fans feel the victory of their team or sports hero as if it is their own. They feel the defeats perhaps even more strongly.

Your fans feel the same way. They want to celebrate your victories with you. Including your fans in your celebrations leads to a greater level of fan engagement and adds to their sense of belonging to the collective group.

Bon Jovi rewarded their Facebook fans with an exclusive video and song when they reached 1 million fans.

Luxury sports car manufacturer Aston Martin is also taking advantage a big milestone to engage their fan base. To celebrate gaining 1 million fans on Facebook, they will crowdsource the build of an Aston Martin car.[26]

The Aston Martin Facebook Page uses a custom landing page as the default tab to explain the celebration and invite fan participation.

> "TO CELEBRATE REACHING ONE MILLION FANS, WE WOULD LIKE TO REWARD OUR COMMUNITY BY BUILDING AN ASTON MARTIN DESIGNED BY **YOU**."

Fans will vote on:

- ☞ Model
- ☞ Design
- ☞ Specifications

Aston Martin will tally the votes and begin building the model, design and specifications with the most votes. To ensure they don't end up building a school bus yellow minivan with lightning bolts down the side, voting options are limited to models, designs and specifications consistent with the Aston Martin luxury brand.

Celebrating together isn't limited to just your achievements. Invite fans to share victories in their life, especially as it relates to the use of your product/service. Encouraging the submission of user generated content like photos, videos, songs or poems is one of the best ways to ignite your fan base.

Celebrate special occasions, seasonal changes and recognized holidays together. Burt's Bees ran an interactive "Tacky Sweater Party" winter holiday promotion. Fans were invited to post a tacky sweater as their profile picture on Facebook. Burt's Bees donated $1 for each picture posted to One Warm Coat, a national organization providing warm coats to those in need.

Think about how you can relate to your fans and how you can celebrate your company, product/service, brand, etc. together.

FORMULATE YOUR GAME PLAN

Take time to answer the following:

1. What type of celebration would your fans enjoy?

_____

_____

2. How can you involve fans in your company's achievements?

_____

_____

3. How will fans benefit from their participation?

_____

_____

4. How will your company celebrate with your fans?

_____

_____

INVITE PARTICIPATION

Online contests and games naturally encourage participation, but how do you invite your fans to comment, like and share other types of content?

The importance of a like, share or comment on Facebook can't be over-stated. A "Like" on Facebook means a fan clicks the "Like" link located directly under a post as if to agree with or endorse the post. A share happens when a fan clicks on the share link and reposts your content on their personal wall. When a fan "comments" on your post, he/she enters the conversation and leaves a specific note about one of your posts.

According to research conducted by Edgerank Checker, a Facebook maximization software company, **a comment is four times more valuable than a like or share**. Edgerank analyzed more than 80,000 posts of a random sample of 5,500+ Facebook Pages during the month of October

2011. From the data collected, they constructed a formula for the impact of likes, shares and comments on Facebook News Feed placement. According to Edgerank Checker, if you want to maximize the exposure of your posts on Facebook, post items that will solicit comments from your fans.

Whether you want your fans to comment on your Facebook Page, Twitter or blog, initiating the conversation is often difficult. Many online visitors only want to look at content instead of engaging with you and speaking up to voice an opinion or share an idea. I call those types of visitors "lurkers" and it can be a challenge to get them to participate.

How can you increase fan participation?

☞ *Call-to-action language.* Use active verbs in your copy like "Click here," "Sign Up Today," and "Act Now." This kind of language is especially important on your corporate website. Ask visitors to buy or request more information. Don't be shy about it. Use a combination of call-to-action language, graphics and tools like Live Chat or Click-to-Call to keep your fans engaged. Include call-to-action language in any graphics designed for your corporate or social site profiles. Fans are more likely to engage when you specifically ask them to do so.

☞ *Give benefits.* Tell your fans the benefit to becoming a fan, sharing content or commenting on your post. In the Burt's Bees "Tacky Sweater Party" campaign, engagement is tied to a charitable donation so there is a tangible benefit to participation. Make sure the benefit is strategic and aligned with your business goals. Occasionally, offer a non-self-serving benefit that either directly benefits the fans or a non-profit organization of your choice.

☞ *Treat comments with respect.* Fans are more likely to comment on your content when they have "social proof" that it's safe to participate. Treat all opinions with respect, unless a comment crosses the line to obscene or profane. You should remove any obscene or profane content or comment immediately.

☞ *Ask a question.* Audience polls are a great way to start your online conversation. Try a combination of multiple choice polls and open ended questions to discover which type engages your audience the most. Don't ask questions about your product/service unless it has a humorous twist. Ask questions that your fans will care about. Try something local to your area like a favorite sports team or an interesting national headline. Stay away from politics and religion unless you want to start a heated debate and/or that type of conversation is congruent with your brand.

☞ *Attention grabbing headlines.* With so much written content on the Internet, a snappy blog title, email subject line, tweet or Facebook post can make all the difference. If you want to improve your headline writing skills, pick up a national newspaper (or use their free app and access it on your iPad) and scan down the page. Which headlines stand out to you? What are the characteristics that make one title grab your eye instead of another? Good headlines use action or power words. They are concise and clearly indicate what the content is about. Good headlines often ask a thought provoking question of interest to the target audience. For corporate websites and blogs, good headlines integrate search marketing keywords to improve your rankings in Google search results. Another trick to writing a good headline is using a number to quantify the information. People want to know what they will learn if they read your content. a number reassures readers of the value in your content.

For an example of killer call-to-action online marketing, look no further than Go Daddy, a domain registrar and website/email hosting provider. From its corporate website, which averages 10 calls-to-action per page, to its Facebook Fan Page, with customized tabs, contests and a $1 domain offer, Go Daddy has mastered the art of calls-to-action. Even its television commercials have a strong call-to-action component; you can't see the end of the commercial (which is teased heavily as something scandalous and naughty) unless you log onto GoDaddy.com.

A recent post on the Go Daddy Facebook Page demonstrates how to include call-to-action in a simple text post.

> *71 Races, 2 Poles, and 30 Top 10 Finishes!*
> *Two years of racing with NASCAR legends Mark Martin and Hendrick Motorsports have been a pleasure! Like to help us say Thank You and post your comments below for both! ^Colby*

Last time I checked, the post received 32 likes and 9 comments, which will lead to higher visibility for the page in the News Feed, according to Edgerank Checker.

Ask you customers to engage and they will, if it benefits them and they value your content.

FORMULATE YOUR GAME PLAN

Take time to answer the following:

1. What action words could you start including in your web copy?

   _____

   _____

   _____

2. Which of your websites need more call-to-action? Which one will you start working on first?

   _____

   _____

   _____

3. How well is your page ranking in the Facebook News Feed? What do you need to do to improve your Edgerank?

   _____

   _____

   _____

MEET UP AND TWEET UP

Most of the tips we've discussed so far focus on engaging your fans in a virtual environment. It's time to talk about the power of in-person events as part of your engagement mix. Open houses, holiday celebrations, customer appreciation gatherings and employee recognition events are great ways to unite fans and solidify loyalty.

Many organizations have started providing value-added education to their fan base as a way to gain new fans and thank existing fans for repeat business. Go Realty in Cary, NC recently hosted a complimentary "iPad Summit" for any real estate agent in the area who wanted to attend. The event was marketed online with a blog and social media. Go Realty also recruited local speakers for the rapid-fire two-hour seminar before the cocktail party. The event was the perfect combination of education and fun and the end result was spectacular. There was standing room only at the event and attendees received a ton of practical, useful information on how to use their iPad more productively to increase sales.

Go Realty's unique event was open to agents from all real estate companies. Many companies provide education to their own sales staff members, but Go Realty decided to take it a step further. They believe that by raising the level of professionalism industry wide, Go Realty agents will benefit in the long run. If a home buyer or seller has a positive experience with a real estate agent in the past, they are much more likely to work with an agent again. The next time might be with a Go Realty agent.

If you are already using in-person events as a way to connect with fans, the next step is to market the event using Internet marketing tools and provide real time updates as the event happens on social media. Marketing your event online is so much more than putting a website address on your brochure. It is important to integrate your event into all of your Internet marketing tools such as your website, email marketing, blog, social media sites and online public relations.

Before you finalize the event marketing, consider the following:

- ☞ Is the online event hub website or webpage easy to find from your main website?
- ☞ Are you marketing to a specific domain name for the event or marketing your main website address?
- ☞ What other online avenues do you plan to use to drive traffic to the event webpage?
- ☞ How often do you plan to post messages or send emails prior to the event?

☞ Do you have a strong call-to-action message on the event webpage that will motivate visitors to sign up for the event or request more information about the event?

☞ Is there a separate webpage for potential sponsors or exhibitors to learn more about participating in the event?

☞ Do you have easy online registration for the event?

If this is a small event and you have a limited budget, I recommend marketing your main website domain name either with a short permalink to the event webpage (i.e. abccompany.com/event) and adding a highly visible graphic to the homepage so the event information is easy to find. For email and social media posts, link directly to the event page instead of your main homepage.

Another low cost option is to create a free blog about the site using blogger.com or wordpress.com. These sites have fantastic free templates to choose from to customize with your logo and graphics. You can also use sites like MeetUp.com and Facebook Event Pages to create a free online presence for the event where attendees can RSVP and post about the event. Simply Google "event rsvp sites" for more online options.

If your event warrants a more professional appearance and is something you plan to host more than once, consider an event website with a custom domain name. This is the best option and will attract more serious attendees with the professional look and feel of the site.

The final step is to engage your fan base with events. Post real time updates from your event on social networking sites like Facebook and Twitter.

Here are several tips to encourage your attendees to tweet before, during and after the event:

- ☞ Before the event, establish a Twitter handle and #hashtag specific to the event.
- ☞ Prior to the event, tweet event updates and announcements.
- ☞ Proactively market the event webpage, Twitter handle and hashtag on all event marketing.
- ☞ Link to the Twitter profile for the event webpage and feed the event tweets to the event webpage.
- ☞ Invite attendees to tweet from the event and provide a hashtag for everyone to use.
- ☞ Provide the twitter handle and hashtag on the event program or guidebook.
- ☞ If using PowerPoint slides, make the Twitter handle and event hashtag part of the background graphic so they're on every slide.
- ☞ Include speakers' Twitter handles in their introductions.
- ☞ Include attendees' Twitter handle on their nametags.
- ☞ Designate a staff member to monitor Twitter during the event to respond to attendees' tweets and retweet in real time.

The benefit to bringing your in-person event to life on social networks is that it will engage fans who couldn't attend and will encourage them to attend next time. If your event receives a negative comment, respond quickly and professionally and move on. You can't please everyone and most fans understand that. It only hurts the event if the comment goes unaddressed.

FORMULATE YOUR GAME PLAN

Take time to answer the following:

1. How can you combine the power of in-person events with Internet marketing before, during and after an event?

   _____

   _____

   _____

2. How can Twitter help you market your next event?

   _____

   _____

   _____

3. Is there a social media-savvy person attending your event who can be the designated tweeter?

   _____

   _____

   _____

PART IV

THE EQUIPMENT

"Do not let what you cannot do interfere with what you can do."

John Wooden
Former Head Coach UCLA Men's Basketball
Won 10 NCAA National Championships

A ny task is infinitely easier if you have the right tools for the job. The world of online marketing is no different. Online marketing can be incredibly tedious and time-consuming if you attempt to do it manually.

Look for tools that offer shortcuts and automate manual processes. You also want tools that are multifunctional and combine multiple processes into one tool.

The following is a list of my favorite online tools that help me be the most productive and effective online marketer I can be:

Social Media Dashboard

I've mentioned this tool several times because I find it indispensable. If you are tired of logging into multiple social media sites each day, a social media dashboard application is the perfect answer. Social media dashboards allow you to monitor and post to multiple social networks, including Facebook and Twitter. Many dashboard options are available, including Hootsuite, Sprout Social, Tweetdeck, Argyle Social and Social Guides. I tried both Tweetdeck and Hootsuite and prefer Hootsuite to Tweetdeck. Hootsuite runs as an online program instead of downloaded software. The Hootsuite dashboard is also much more visually appealing and the ability to pre-schedule posts is a life-saver. Hootsuite has a free version and a pro version available for $5.99/month. I use the $5.99 version because I want all the bells and whistles at a price that's very affordable.

After you set up your dashboard account, enter the log-in and password for each of your social network profiles in the account. Hootsuite auto-matically pulls the feed from each site and allows you to monitor and update each site from one central dashboard.

Some marketers have expressed concern about using a third party application to post on Facebook because of the Edgerank algorithm (Facebook's formula that ranks objects in the Facebook News Feed). It was reported that posting from a third party app, like Hootsuite, will lower your Edgerank score and your posts will appear in a lesser prominent position in the News Feed. But according to a recent tweet by Matt Trainer, developer consultant to Facebook, "This should be fixed. Thanks for your patience. We are always making changes to our News Feed algorithm. We recently made a fix that added more signals to detect good quality posting behavior. This should improve the situation with the distribution of posts coming from third-party apps in the News Feed."[27]

The free Hootsuite app also allows you to "hoot" on-the-go from your smartphone or tablet, making it even easier to keep up with your social networking profiles. What a hoot!

Twitter

You may find this suggestion surprising since Twitter is mainly used as a marketing and communication tool, but it is also a fantastic research tool. I routinely monitor Twitter for mentions of my brand so I can appropriately respond. I also monitor Twitter for industry news, trends and content research. Twitter is the most efficient social networking tool of all of the tools available because posts must be 140 characters or less. Twitter's concise nature forces communication to be more to the point. You can also create lists by topic, industry or keyword to easily monitor specific conversations. If you use a social media dashboard product, you can conveniently keep up with your Twitter feed.

Email Marketing System

Even the smallest business needs email marketing software. Don't send your bulk email campaigns from an email client like Outlook or Gmail. These programs are most likely sent straight to your recipients' junk/spam folder. Instead, send all group or bulk email correspondence from an email service provider like Constant Contact, iContact, Emma, Vertical Response, COMF5 and Jango Mail. I personally use Constant Contact, iContact, and COMF5 depending on the client's needs. Constant Contact has the most pre-designed templates and also carries shopping cart integration. iContact recently rolled out social media dashboard integration to manage and monitor your social media from the same platform as your email marketing software. Now that's convenient! COMF5's strong point is the ability to embed video messages that you record using COMF5 in email. All of the products mentioned here are priced comparably based on the number of subscribers on your email list. All of these products also allow you to embed a custom email sign-up form on your corporate website, blog, or Facebook Page so new subscribers are fed automatically to your list.

Most of these DIY-friendly programs offer ready-made templates and custom designs. Be prepared for the learning curve when using the editor to populate and edit your content. With patience and training you can learn how to create your own branded email campaigns. These email marketing programs also offer campaign tracking tools to help you determine how many people opened the campaign, clicked on links in the email, shared the email on social sites, unsubscribed and reported the email as spam. Check your tracking reports frequently to quantify your degree of fan engagement.

Depending on the size of your email subscriber list and the amount of email marketing you plan to do, you may need a more robust tool like

Exact Target, Bronto Mail or Silver Pop. These platforms generally have a start-up fee of a couple thousand dollars and a nominal per email fee for every email you send. If that seems expensive, keep in mind the robust nature of these tools will be worth every penny because you can automate manual tasks and report in-depth data on more complex campaigns.

App Store

I love the app store almost as much as I love Bon Jovi (if Bon Jovi had an app, it would be the perfect combination!). Take a moment the next time you are stuck in the airport or watching mindless reality television to browse through the app store on your smartphone or tablet. I like to browse the "Featured" apps to see what's new in the app world. I also like to search by categories, specifically the Business, Finance, Lifestyle, News, and Social categories. I also frequently type a task that I wish to simplify into the search feature of the app store and browse available apps to automate a manual task. I love free apps, but I am willing to pay if the app appears to truly help me become more productive or effective.

Some of my favorite and most helpful apps include (in alphabetical order):

- ☞ Call a Taxi
- ☞ Dragon
- ☞ Dropbox
- ☞ Facebook
- ☞ Faces
- ☞ Fandango
- ☞ Find iPhone
- ☞ FlightTrack
- ☞ Flipboard
- ☞ GateGuru
- ☞ GoDaddy
- ☞ Google Maps
- ☞ Gorillacam
- ☞ Groupon
- ☞ Hootsuite
- ☞ i-Clickr
- ☞ iContact
- ☞ iHeartRadio
- ☞ Instagram
- ☞ KeyRing
- ☞ LinkedIn
- ☞ Point Inside
- ☞ QR Reader
- ☞ Quicklytics
- ☞ Scanner
- ☞ Shutterfly
- ☞ Square
- ☞ Swipe
- ☞ TripAdvisor
- ☞ TripIt Pro
- ☞ TWC
- ☞ UF Football
- ☞ USA Today
- ☞ Where To Eat
- ☞ White Noise
- ☞ World Card Mobile

When the television commercial says "There's an app for that"—there really is! There are more than half a million apps for the iPhone alone. Tap into the power of apps and you can make your personal and professional world so much more productive and pleasant.

Professional Writer

You may not think of suggesting using a professional writer as a tool per se, but I can assure you that a reliable professional copywriter who understands your brand and can write with an authentic tone for you is a lifesaver. We've already talked about the need for outsourcing and I can't stress enough how much hiring a proficient writer as an employee or an independent contractor can mean to your business. Words are the currency of the new millennium. You must either hire staff members who are competent writers or hire someone to professionally write your communications.

Screen Capture/Image Editor

I absolutely could not make it through a single day without my screen capture/image editor software. I use it to grab images from websites we are developing to show the designer or developer the error I am seeing, to grab screenshot images for power point presentations and to resize images I plan to use on a website or social media site. There are many of these tools available; simply Google "Screen Capture" or "Image Editor" and you will find a wide variety of free and paid software options. The program I prefer is called SnagIt by TechSmith. I've used this tool for years and prefer its ease of navigation and robust nature. At the time of printing, Techsmith offered a 30 day free trial, after which time Snagit cost $49.95 USD to purchase. SnagIt is downloadable software for your computer, so if anything happens to your computer or you upgrade to a new computer, you have to purchase the program again.

Whatever tool you purchase, make sure it has the ability to crop, resize and grab screenshots. In most cases, if your images look pixelated or load slowly on the web, your graphics aren't sized properly. Ask your webmaster what the standard image sizes for your website are so you can size all images consistently. Your website will look much more professional and load much faster. Image sizes are defined by pixels. For a horizontal (landscape) image, the important measurement is the width. For vertical (portrait) images, the important measurement is the height. If you are resizing a horizontal image, adjust the size for the width and allow the height to automatically adjust proportionately to the new width dimension.

A screen capture/image editing tool is also very helpful with your email campaigns. You can screenshot email drafts so your designer can see how the campaign will appear in your email client's inbox. You can also mark up an image with notes and show exactly what changes you want the designer to make. Screen capture programs make the editing process much faster. Some programs will also capture video images of your screen with audio and recordings. This is especially helpful if you work on a projects with someone not located in your office.

Stock Photos

Don't run the risk of grabbing images from Google Image search and using them in your marketing. In most cases, the images are protected by a copyright, so you may be committing copyright infringement by using them. For specific legal do's and don'ts of using images from the web, consult your attorney. The best way to avoid any copyright issues is to purchase royalty-free stock photos. My favorite stock photo sites are Fotolia, Shutterstock and iStockPhoto. Web-friendly images on these sites generally run $10—$15 each. You can also buy a collection of photos on a CD if you like a particular photographer, model or topic. Search by keyword on the sites to find photos appropriate for your project. The

163

more specific your search, the better the results. If searching for photos with people, you can specify age, ethnicity, gender and sexual orientation. When I need more artistic photos, I visit Getty Images. They are more expensive, typically starting at $50+ (depending on the size of the image). Before you purchase an image, determine where and how you plan to use it. You want to make sure you purchase the right size. Ask your graphic designer if unsure about a specific size. If you are still unsure, purchase one size larger than you think you will need. You can always size an image down and maintain the image quality. You can't make an image larger without affecting the quality.

FORMULATE YOUR GAME PLAN

Take time to answer the following:

1. Take an inventory of your technology and software tools. Which one(s) are working for you? Which one(s) are hard to use and not working effectively?

2. What tools do you need to acquire during the next year to work more productively?

3. What is your plan to learn more about effectively using technology tools and resources?

4. What resources are available to help you stay up to speed on emerging tools and trends?

PART V

THE SCORE

"To succeed...You need to find something to hold on to, something to motivate you and something to inspire you."

Tony Dorsett
Retired NFL Running Back
Pro & College Football Hall of Fame Inductee

Just like referees keep track of the score during a football, basketball, or soccer game, you must keep score of your online sales and marketing efforts. Marketing can be a very subjective topic if you focus only on aesthetic issues like color or design style preferences. Another common mistake is assuming your web surfing and social networking preferences apply to everyone else. Everyone "clicks" a little differently and it's important not to assume your tastes apply to your customers.

Have you ever wondered:

- ☞ How do I know if my online sales and marketing efforts are working?
- ☞ How do I judge the effectiveness of a Facebook contest, email campaign or blog post?
- ☞ How much should I budget and what is the return on my investment?

All of these questions are answered with analytics. **Monitoring your website and social sites with analytics is a must for the serious marketer.** Without objective feedback on the results of your efforts, you are essentially driving blind though the fog while throwing money out the window of the car.

I recommend the following monitoring tools:

- ☞ Google Analytics (for your website or blog)
- ☞ Facebook Insights
- ☞ Email Marketing Reports
- ☞ Twitter Reports

If you use a dashboard program like Hootsuite, you can access all of your reporting in one account, including the items mentioned above (except the email marketing reports). This is very handy and makes monitoring activity quick and easy.

If you prefer to access Google Analytics directly, you can schedule an email report delivered automatically, which is a simple way to remember to review the numbers. Google Analytics allows you to custom design your report dashboard and will show only the information of interest to you. Don't jump to any conclusions about your numbers until you've gathered at least six months of data and established a baseline for your site.

The following reports in Google Analytics offer a good deal of insight:

☞ *Visitors Overview*—This report gives you an idea of the health of your website. It measures the number of visits, unique visitors, page views, number of pages viewed per visit, average time spent on site, bounce rate and percentage of new visits.

☞ *Demographics/Location*—This report shows you where your web visitors are coming from by country, city, continent and sub-continent. If you plan any local marketing, this tool is incredibly helpful in helping you identify where you should be marketing.

☞ *Behavior*—There are three reports in this series: New vs. Returning, Frequency & Recency, and Engagement. These reports measure how engaged visitors are with your site and how often they return.

☞ *Social Engagement*—This report is available in the new version of Google Analytics, which will soon be the default version. This report measures the level of social engagement on your site.

☞ *Mobile*—This report measures the percentage of visitors accessing your site from a mobile device and what mobile devices were used.

☞ *Traffic Sources*—This report analyzes where your website traffic came from. Being able to see which sources are actually producing traffic is critical if you spend money on advertising.

☞ *Content*—This report analyzes which pages are popular on your website as well as how visitors click through your website.

☞ *Conversions*—Track visitor actions on your site, such as video downloads, email sign-ups, or ecommerce sales.

☞ *Real Time*—The Real Time report allows you to see how many visitors are on your website at that moment, including which pages are being viewed and where the traffic came from. Amazing! Real Time reporting allows you to monitor the immediate impact of a social media posts or email campaigns. Post your message and then login into your Google Analytics account to watch the traffic pour in.

Google Analytics reporting is all web-based so you can log in 24/7/365 to review your reports. If you outsource your website maintenance, make sure the webmaster gives you the Google Analytic username and password for your records. The glossary and help center are very detailed and easy to understand. You can also post a question and ask for help. Other users may know the answer and post a response to your question. **Review Google Analytics with a professional online marketing consultant or your webmaster on a monthly basis. After six months of data you can begin to draw meaningful conclusions about the performance of your website or blog.**

Facebook Insights

What is the value of a "Like?" Social media strategists frequently argue and speculate on the answer to this question. Some even place a dollar figure on it. **The truth is the value of a "like" is vastly different from business to business.** The value of a new "like" on a celebrity's Facebook Page is completely different than a new "like" on a small business' page. Not only is the value of a "like" different, but what the fans want in terms of content is also very different. How often to post and what to post is contingent upon the type of page you have and the audience it reaches.

Monitoring your Facebook Insights report is an excellent way to measure the effectiveness of your page and receive valuable feedback on what your audience wants. The Insights Report is accessed by page administrators by clicking on the Insights link located in the left column navigation under your profile image.

If you are new to reviewing Facebook Insights, there is a helpful user guide that explains how to interpret the reports. You can access the user guide by clicking on the [⚙ ▾] button next to the Export Data button on the main dashboard report. The Export Data feature allows you to pick any date range and export the data to an excel file (.xls) or comma separated value file (.csv).

Four reports are available: Likes, Reach, Talking About This and Check-Ins.

☞ *Likes*—This report shows you the total number of likes or fans of your Page. It also tells you the number of "Friends of Fans," which is the number of unique people who are friends of your fans. The Friends of Fans report displays your potential reach if all your fans recruited their network to be your fan. "People Talking About This" reports the number of people who created a story about your page in the last seven days and the "Weekly Total Reach" reports the number of unique people who saw any content associated with your Page in the last seven days. This report also tracks your number of "unlikes" in a given time period, which is also very important to watch. If you see a spike of "unlikes," look back at what you posted and how often you post to determine how you can improve your post behaviors to engage more fans.

☞ *Reach*—This report shows you the demographic information of your fans, such as age range, gender and location. You can learn how you reached fans either through organic, viral or paid marketing on Facebook and which part of your page was viewed, such as the wall, photos or information links.

☞ *Talking About This*—You can find this number in the left column of your page underneath your total number of fans. It reflects the number of people who created a story about your page within the given date range. A story is created when someone "likes" your page, posts to your page wall, or comments on a post. For the complete list of what counts as a story, see the user guide. The Insight report goes into more detail on the number of people talking about your page and adds demographic and location information if you have more than 30 people talking about your page.

☞ *Check-ins*—If your business has a physical location customers can visit, this insight records the number of people who checked in on Facebook while attending your location. Again, if you have more than 30 people checked in, you can also track demographic and location information on the people who checked in.

How do you interpret the Facebook data? Like your website analytics, gather at least six months of data before you draw any positive or negative conclusions. Then look for patterns to emerge.

- ☞ What type of post(s) garners the most likes, comments or shares from your audience?
- ☞ Is there a frequency threshold that keeps your audience engaged, but doesn't result in unlikes?
- ☞ Are demographic or location trends useful to your traditional marketing strategy?

You may have more questions than answers the first few times you review the Facebook Insights report. The answers will become evident in time if you consistently review the reports and apply common sense. If you still feel unsure of what your fans want, ask them! Use focus groups, surveys and polls to receive feedback from your fans. To elicit the most feedback possible, offer a benefit or incentive to participate. It's good to check in with your fans regularly to see if you are meeting their needs. However, don't ask too often. Your fans don't mind giving you feedback, but they also feel you should know what motivates them to engage. Since fans strongly identify with you and your brand, they expect you to do the same for them. Asking too many redundant or obvious questions about what they want to see on your Facebook Page will turn them off.

Email Reports

If you send email campaigns on a frequent basis, be sure to review the email campaign reports so you can tweak subsequent campaigns for maximum impact. Before drawing any conclusions on the performance of your campaign, first research reasonable email marketing benchmarks for your industry. MailChimp.com has an excellent library of resources, including benchmark studies by industry and business size. These reports give you an indication if you are average, above average or below average and need improvement within your industry or business size.

- ☞ *Open Rate*—This is the number of recipients who opened the email. Some email marketing programs also report on the Unique Open Rate, which is the number of unique individuals who opened the campaign. This number eliminates duplicates and gives you a more realistic picture of how many people actually opened the campaign.

- ☞ *Bounce Rate*—This is the number of recipients who did not receive the email. Sometimes mail servers send the email back with a message that it could not be delivered. There are two types of bounces: soft and hard. Soft bounces occur when a mail server temporarily cannot deliver an email because the recipient's email inbox is full or the server is down. A hard bounce occurs when the mail server permanently cannot deliver the email because the email address no longer exists or the email address is not valid.

- ☞ *Click Rate*—This is the ratio of clicks to the number of recipients. Clicks are generated when a recipient clicks on a link in the email and visits your website, blog or social media site.

- ☞ *Complaints*—This is the number of recipients who reported your email as spam to their email service provider.

174

☞ *Unsubscribe*—This is the number of recipients who asked to be removed from your email list.

Generally speaking, you want a larger open rate and a smaller bounce rate. An email list with a low open rate indicates your content is either not relevant to the target audience, the email subject line sounds like spam and/or you are sending email too frequently.

A high bounce rate is usually a sign of an old, stale email list. Email service providers tend to mark campaigns with high bounce rates as spam and cause the email to go into the recipients spam or junk folder. Monitor your bounce rate and clean hard bounces out of your system on a regular basis. Mail Chimp recommends you keep soft bounces in your account, but after 5 soft bounces remove them from your list as well.

You should also strive for a large click-through rate. A high click-through rate means the content is interesting and the recipient wants to know more about the topic or your organization. The more links in your email, the higher the click-through rate becomes since you offer more opportunities to click. Be sure to include links to all of your online marketing, including your blog and social media profiles. Email is the most effective way to drive traffic and cross promote your website, blog and social media profiles.

The complaints number and unsubscribe number should be very low. Most email marketing programs do not allow more than one or two abuse complaints per campaign. If you have a large number, they will shut down your account until you prove that the list is permission-based and that you have taken steps to clean up your list. Spam complaints typically come from free email accounts such as Hotmail, Yahoo Mail and Gmail since they have a prominent spam complaint button on the inbox dashboard. Microsoft Outlook users have to take more steps to report an email as spam. If your list is permission-based, it is possible that any abuse complaints are an error. Perhaps the recipient forgot they opted in to receive the email or didn't recognize your name. To prevent false reports, make sure your email subject line clearly states what the email is about and the "from" name on the email clearly states the sender's name.

A high unsubscribe rate indicates you are sending email too frequently; the content is not interesting and/or not relevant to your audience.

Don't worry if you have an occasional poor response to an email campaign. As long as the trend doesn't continue, it won't have a long-term effect. However, if you don't monitor your results and several campaigns perform poorly, you could be blacklisted by email service providers, damaging your ability to deliver email to your customers and clients.

Twitter Reports

Twitter.com offers three helpful reports you can use to manage your Twitter account. The "@Username" (insert your username after the "@" sign) report displays all of the mentions you receive on Twitter. Review this report at least once a day if you're actively tweeting. It's the best way to find out if someone mentions your brand name in the Twitterverse so you can take appropriate action. If you are larger company, you may also want to solicit the services of a reputation management program that will automatically notify you by email of any mentions. Refer back to Secret #6 for more information on this topic.

The Activity report shows the actions of people you follow, such as new connections, retweets and favorites, and helps you find others with similar interests to follow. Similarly, the "Who to Follow" report offers suggestions of Twitter profiles that might interest you based on who you currently follow and who follows you.

176

In addition to the reports offered for free on Twitter.com and Facebook.com, you can also generate reports from your social media dashboard software. One report I particularly like is Hootsuite's "Ow.ly Summary Stats" report, which shows you how many clicks you receive on links embedded in your tweets. This report also shows you where the clicks come from, such as Twitter.com, third party apps on smartphones, Facebook, or Hootsuite.com users. If you monitor the number of clicks your tweets receive, you can identify what language, tone and topics resonate with your audience.

Information Overload

WOW! That's a lot of reporting. If you feel a bit overwhelmed right now, don't worry. You aren't alone. It's a lot to digest, even for online marketing professionals who monitor website activity and social media metrics as part of their day-to-day work. Running the reports, reviewing the data and drawing cohesive conclusions requires experience and broad-based knowledge. This is where an Internet marketing consultant or webmaster can assist you. Professional Internet marketers can explain the reports in laymen's terms and make sense of the numbers. If you don't feel your webmaster or marketing manager does that effectively, hire additional help. Your fans won't be fans for long if you don't feed them the content they crave. And, you can't know what they crave if you don't have accurate, informative feedback.

If you hire a professional marketer to assist you, make sure routine reporting and review sessions are part of the marketing package. The marketing company should proactively provide the reporting each month and make it easy for you to access the information directly. It is your information! Document all the username and passwords to your reporting accounts and maintain the master account in-house. If you part ways with the marketing company, you don't want them taking your account history with them.

Lastly, be aware that the reports do change frequently. Just about the time you become comfortable with what a report is measuring and how to interpret it, the report changes. Some changes are just minor tweaks and others are total overhauls. The reporting website's glossary and user guide can help you become familiar with the changes. In the Resources section, I list a number of sites that can help keep you up-to-date on the latest and greatest in the world of online marketing.

FORMULATE YOUR GAME PLAN

Take time to answer the following:

1. What Internet sales and marketing reports are you currently reviewing? How often?

   _____

   _____

   _____

2. Out of the reports mentioned in this report, which one do you not currently review that would be helpful to your business?

   _____

   _____

   _____

3. What steps do you need to take to implement additional reporting and review sessions?

   _____

   _____

   _____

CONCLUSION

I saved the best secret to increase fan engagement for last. It's *passion*. **If you have an unbridled passion for your product, service, industry or customers you will create an unbreakable bond between you and your fans.**

Business owners, marketers and salespeople with passion can break a few of the rules and still maintain a great relationship with their fans. Passion overrides textbook tactics. Conversely, without passion you can implement the other 20 secrets and fall short of engaging your fans. Ultimately, fans need to know you love and care about them as much as they care about you. Your passion for the fans will demonstrate that emotion far better than the perfect tweet, the most creative Facebook contest or killer email campaign.

I define passion as energy. People who are passionate about their career, product or service ooze energy out of every pore. It feels good to be around them. They inspire you to think bigger and leave you feeling invigorated. Passion is an intangible quality that you know when you see.

Think about the people you've met over the years. Does anyone stand out as a bundle of passionate energy? How does that person make you feel? Do you look forward to seeing or talking to that person on a regular basis? Do you follow them on social networks hoping to pick up nuggets of inspiration?

Here's the thing about passion—you may feel it but it takes a conscious decision to share it with others.

- ☞ It means on the days that you don't feel especially passionate, you still attend a networking event and when you get there you don't stand in the corner complaining about your woes to people you know while ignoring potential new contacts.

- ☞ It means that even when you are incredibly busy with your own challenges and struggles you still make time to post an educational article on your blog.

- ☞ It means when you are absolutely too busy to even sleep, you still make time to wish fans Happy Birthday on Facebook or email a colleague through LinkedIn.

- ☞ It means in your most challenging hour when you would love to vent and post an angry rant about someone or something online, you hold back and keep it to yourself.

If you have been working a long time you may feel burned out by the daily grind. If time off or a change in diet and exercise doesn't resolve that feeling, then it's time to move on. If you've "lost that loving feeling" for your product or service, there's no way you can build and maintain a rabid fan base.

It's possible to maintain passion over a long career and stressful circumstances. Think about the legendary rock stars like Bono of U2 who have been performing for stadiums packed full of screaming fans for over 30 years. How does he do that? Doesn't he get tired? Of course! But in the end his love of the fans, the music and thrill of performing outweighs the sore throats, audio-visual headaches and the travel nightmares that come with a world tour.

No one's job is easy. Some jobs may look more glamorous than others, but work is called work because, well frankly, it's work.

Fun is called fun because it's fun. Sometimes work is fun but sometimes it's just work.

Why do we do it? Because of what my dad calls "the glory in the daily grind." If you love what you do and you know that it makes a difference to your fans, you can tackle any task, obstacle or challenge with grace and passion.

RESOURCES (ALPHA ORDER)

Websites & Blogs

CNN Tech
ConvinceandConvert.com
eMarketer.com
Entrepreneur.com
Forbes Tech
GoogleBlog.Blogspot.com
Hubspot.com
IgniteSocialMedia.com

Kaushik.net/avinash
MarketingProfs.com
Mashable.com
OpenForum.com
SearchEngineLand.com
SocialMediaExaminer.com
TheDigitalDivaBlog.com
USA Today Tech

Who to Follow on Twitter

@BrianSolis
@ChrisBrogan
@CreatingWOW
@GaryVee
@GinaCarr

@GinaSchreck
@GuyKawasaki
@KimGarst
@MariSmith
@TimOReilly

HAVE MEREDITH OLIVER
SPEAK AT YOUR NEXT EVENT!

Meredith Oliver is a professional speaker and during the past ten years, she has given hundreds of presentations to a variety of audiences—always to rave reviews!

Meredith delivers:
- ☞ Keynote speeches
- ☞ In-person sales training seminars
- ☞ Web seminar sales training
- ☞ Convention/conference break-out sessions
- ☞ Banquet hosting & event emcee
- ☞ Association programs
- ☞ Continuing education programs

"AWESOME JOB! Meredith you were awesome on Friday. The program went smoothly and we had standing room only. I appreciate all you do and look forward to many years of knowing you and hearing feature seminars."—**Cindy Nugent Huber, StructSure Home Warranty**

"What a pleasure meeting you, and what an awesome presentation! Thanks so much for making our WOAMTEC Confident Women's Conference such a huge success. I certainly look forward to seeing you again. You are truly an inspiration to all women!"—**Sherry Shaw, My Shopping Genie**

Connect With Meredith!

CreatingWOW.com
TheDigitalDivaBlog.com
@CreatingWOW
Facebook.com/meredith.oliver
YouTube.com/mereditholivertv
linkedin.com/in/mereditholiver

CLICK POWER: THE PROVEN SYSTEM TO INCREASE SALES

Awebsite with no Web marketing is like a billboard in the Everglades. It doesn't exist.

Just because you developed a website doesn't mean Web shoppers can find it—or when they do find it, that they'll take action. Building a website is only the first step of an effective Internet marketing strategy.

The **Click Power System**™ is a roadmap to increase sales with an effective online sales and marketing program. The system outlines five building blocks:

1. Your Website Design—The Foundation
2. Website Marketing—Drive Traffic
3. eLead Follow-Up—Build the Relationship
4. Online Onsite Marriage—Close the Sale
5. Measure Results—Track, Review & Revise

If you want to stop wasting time and money on marketing tactics that do not produce results, order your copy of *Click Power* today and watch your business soar!

www.CreatingWOW.com

CLICK-BY-CLICK "HOW-TO" TUTORIALS
BY MEREDITH OLIVER

Seven Deadly Sins of Social Media

Learn how to avoid key, embarrassing and potentially reputation-damaging mistakes in social media networking. The Seven Deadly Sins are outlined with examples and will teach you how often to post and what to post. This tutorial is a LIVE recording of Meredith's standing room only seminar with screenshots and power point. Total run time 110 minutes. Delivered on a 2 gig USB flash drive. Just plug and play.

Learn to Love LinkedIn

Learn how to set-up, maintain and maximize a personal and group profile on LinkedIn. Discover the best practices for building your connections, finding new connections and interacting with your connections. Learn how to update your status, add applications like SlideShare and give/receive recommendations. Total run time 74 minutes. Delivered on a 2 gig USB flash drive. Just plug and play.

Face Up to Facebook

Learn how to set-up, maintain and maximize a personal profile, business page, event page, networked blog page and group page. Discover the best practices for building your brand and networking with the power of Facebook. Divided into 4 segments. Total run time 122 minutes. Delivered on a 2 gig USB flash drive. Just plug and play.

Click! Social Media Strategy Tutorial

Based on a popular seminar by Meredith Oliver, this self-paced tutorial teaches you how to develop an effective social media strategy in 7 easy steps. Meredith uses real life examples and case studies to demonstrate how to market yourself or your company on the Internet using social media like Facebook, Twitter, LinkedIn, Wordpress, Blogger and YouTube. Detailed learning guide included. Divided into 5 short segments. Total run time 143 minutes. Delivered on a 2 gig USB flash drive. Just plug and play.

Order today at www.CreatingWOW.com

ENDNOTES

1   McGee, Matt. "By the Numbers: Twitter vs. Facebook vs. Google Buzz." Search engine land. 23 Feb. 2010.
    http://searchengineland.com/by-the-numbers-twitter-vs-facebook-vs-google-buzz-36709.

2   McGee, Matt. "By the Numbers: Twitter vs. Facebook vs. Google Buzz." Search engine land. 23 Feb. 2010.
    http://searchengineland.com/by-the-numbers-twitter-vs-facebook-vs-google-buzz-36709.

3   De Kunder, Maurice. "The Size of the World Wide Web." Daily Estimated Size of the World Wide Web. http://www.worldwidewebsize.com/. (24 May 2011.)

4   "Exabyte." Wikipedia 19 December 11. http://en.wikipedia.org/wiki/Exabyte

5   "Exabyte." Search Storage 19 December 11.
    http://searchstorage.techtarget.com/definition/exabyte.

6   Phillips, Lisa E. "Trends in Consumers' Time Spent With Media." eMarketer. 28 Dec. 2010.
    http://www.emarketer.com/(X(1)S(nl3svt45ztjlmimixmtajp55))/Article.aspx?R=10
    08138&AspxAutoDetectCookieSupport=1.

7   Walsh, Mark. "Pew: 35% of American Adults have Smartphones." Media Post News. 11 Jul. 2011.
    http://www.mediapost.com/publications/?fa=Articles.showArticle&art_aid=153864.

8   McKinsey Quarterly, July 2011

9   Cohen, Elizabeth. "Does Life Online Give You 'Popcorn Brain'?". CNN Health. 23 Jun. 2011.
    http://www.cnn.com/2011/HEALTH/06/23/tech.popcorn.brain.ep/index.
    html?hpt=hp_c1.

10 "Media multitasking." Wikipedia. 26 Oct. 2011.
    http://en.wikipedia.org/wiki/Media_multitasking.

11 "Media Multitasking is Really Multi-Distracting." Science Daily. 2 May 2011.
    http://www.sciencedaily.com/releases/2011/05/110502084444.htm.

12 "Swing vote." Wikipedia. 11 Nov. 2011. http://en.wikipedia.org/wiki/Swing_vote.

13 Dowd, Matthew. "Karl Rove—The Architect." UNC TV Frontline. 12 Apr. 2005.
    http://www.pbs.org/wgbh/pages/frontline/shows/architect/interviews/dowd.
    html#ixzz1SPUnoIKT.

14 Dannen, Chris. "How Obama Won It With The Web." Fast Company. 4 Nov. 2008.
    http://www.fastcompany.com/articles/2008/11/how-obama-won-it-with-the-web.html.

15 Ashish, Dev. "Sports Fan Psychology: It's More Than Just A Game." Bleacher Report. 26
    Sept. 2008.
    http://bleacherreport.com/articles/61709-sports-fan-psychology-its-more-than-just-
    a-game.

16 McKinley, Jr., James C. "Sports Psychology; It Isn't Just A Game: Clues to Avid Root-
    ing." The New York Times. 11 Aug. 2000.
    http://www.nytimes.com/2000/08/11/sports/sports-psychology-it-isn-t-just-a-game-
    clues-to-avid-rooting.html.

17 Nielsen, Jakob. "Fancy Words, Fancy Formatting = Looks Like a Promotion = Ignored."
    Use It Alertbox. 4 Sept. 2007.
    http://www.useit.com/alertbox/fancy-formatting.html.

18 Dunkin' Donuts Launches New Advertising Campaign to Celebrate the Passion of
    Real Fans: 'I'm Drinkin' Dunkin'!'." Dunkin' Donuts. 3 Jan. 2011.
    http://news.dunkindonuts.com/dunkin+donuts/dunkin+donuts+news/
    dunkin+donuts+new+ad+campaign.htm.

19 Parr, Ben. "Twitter Surpasses 200 Million Tweets Per Day." Mashable Social Media. 30
    Jun. 2011.
    http://mashable.com/2011/06/30/twitter-200-million/.

20 Hanelly, Andrew. "3 Simple Social Media Lessons from the Bronx Zoo Cobra." Engage
    The Blog. 15 Apr. 2011.

http://engage.tmgcustommedia.com/2011/04/3-simple-social-media-lessons-from-the-bronx-zoo-cobra/.

21 Beal, Andy. "The 4-Hour Social Media Workweek." American Express Open Forum. 15 Sept. 2011.
http://www.openforum.com/articles/the-4-hour-social-media-workweek?intlink=us-openf-nav-gallery.

22 Carroll, Gigi. "American Millennials: The Choice Generation." December 2008.
http://www.draftfcb.com/content/engage/pdf/Engage_Carroll_Dec08.pdf

23 Anderson, Chris and Wolff, Michael. "The Web is Dead. Long Live the Internet." Wired Magazine. 17 August 2010.
http://www.wired.com/magazine/2010/08/ff_webrip/all/1

24 "Viva Glam." M.A.C. http://www.maccosmetics.com/cms/giving_back/vivaglam.tmpl.

25 Schwartz, Ariel. "The Lady Gaga Effect: Pop Star's Social Media Savvy Helps the MAC AIDS Fund Raise Millions of Bucks." Fast Company. 18 Feb. 2011.
http://www.fastcompany.com/1728820/lady-gagas-social-media-savvy-helps-the-mac-aids-fund-raise-millions.

26 Ernst, Kurt. "To Celebrate 1 Million Facebook Fans, Aston Martin Crowdsources A Car." Motor Authority. 14 Nov. 2011.
http://www.motorauthority.com/news/1068605_to-celebrate-1-million-facebook-fans-aston-martin-crowdsources-a-car.

27 Fennell, Tammy Kahn. "Facebook Stops Penalizing 3rd Party Apps In Newsfeed, 'Quality Most Important'." Social Media Today. 10 Nov. 2011.
http://socialmediatoday.com/marketmesuite/385231/facebook-stops-penalizing-3rd-party-apps-newsfeed-quality-most-important.

CPSIA information can be obtained at www.ICGtesting.com
Printed in the USA
BVOW012128150412

287607BV00005B/6/P